WITCH

FOR THOSE WHO ARE

Pre-dawn, midwinter solstice,
with COVEN, Whites Beach, NSW, 1991

LY DE ANGELES

Every book... has a soul. The soul of the person who wrote it and of those who read it and lived and dreamed with it. Every time a book changes hands, every time someone runs his eyes down its pages, its spirit grows and strengthens.

<u>Carlos Ruis Zafon</u>

ALSO BY DE ANGELES —

The Way of the Goddess, Prism/Unity, 1987

The Way of Merlyn, Prism/Unity, 1990

Witchcraft Theory and Practice, Llewellyn Worldwide, 2000

When I See the Wild God, Llewellyn Worldwide, 2002

Pagan Visions, Llewellyn Worldwide, 2004

The Quickening, Llewellyn Worldwide, 2005

The Shining Isle, Llewellyn Worldwide, 2006

Tarot Theory and Practice, Llewellyn Worldwide, 2007

The Quickening, Revised, Createspace 2012

The Shining Isle, Revised, Createspace, 2012

Priteni, the Decimation of the Indigenous Celtic Britons, 2015

Initiation, a Memoir, Createspace, 2016

The Skellig, Science Fiction, Createspace, 2017

WITCH

For Those Who Are – © 2018 Ly de Angeles.

All rights reserved. No part of this book may be used, reproduced, stored in a retrieval system or transmitted in any form or by any means, electronic, mechanical, photocopying, scanning, recording, including Internet usage, without written permission from the author except in the case of brief quotations embodied in critical articles and reviews.

ISBN 9780648502517

Cover design – The Albion Lestrange Family
Ly de Angeles www.lydeangeles.com

Produced by IngramSpark

WITCH

FOR THOSE WHO ARE

INTRODUCTION

WITCHCRAFT CAN BE PRESUMED TO BE as old as humanity. In the caves of Lascaux, France, are the paintings of the hunt. On the tundra of Siberia, the shaman summons a soul back into the ill person and they do not die. The Northern Paiute introduced the Ghost Dance to reunite the living with the dead to achieve the numbers necessary to defeat the invaders. In Australia an Illapurinja, a woman kurdaitcha, will point the bone, bringing about a death to avenge a wrong.

In *Initiation, a Memoir* is written –

Witch people, like magicians and sorcerers, conjurers, druids and hoodoo hexers, like cunning women and cunning men, kurdaitchas, shamans, manitous, angakoks, curanderas, bruxas, noadis, enchanters and shapechangers are needed in this world. We are the stories not bound by dogma or displayed as relics in a museum. We cause disquiet. We summon questions but it's not our way to give answers. We take you to the wild and the frightening places. The cave entrance under the ice at the base of that crevasse. Show you ancient relatives' blue handprints on the rock face imprinted with an ochre of confusion. We are people who cannot be named and from a time you cannot confirm. Once Upon a Time people. People of the reindeer. Volcano people.

Witchcraft could be said to be a generic word. I'll agree to that. Some of you may not. Much hype has gone into proving the validity of tradition or the rightness of its religiosity. I want none of this anymore. It is unnecessary. All the so-called sources are guesses. Fabrications. Invented to confer identity. You, reading this, were likely attracted by the title, or have been given the book by someone who knows you to be witch.

I don't box myself as *a* witch. Not now. Not at this wizened cycle of life because *a* and *the* objectify what is a doing and being self, they are not titles.

We're a little like renegade thoroughbred horses, aren't we? Demanded by our owners to wear the hobbles to become trotters? When we are brumbies and wild mustangs at heart. Free, high country thunderers upon the landscape of a collective consciousness. A memory.

Many years ago, when I was still practicing at becoming witch, I worked ritual and initiated others. I called the practice *witchcraft*, and even titled one of my books *Witchcraft Theory and Practice*. But it was, after all, a practice. A learning to become. That took letting go of an eventually-recognized, unnecessary and vulgar externalization and attachment to androcentrism. It instead required communication with grandmother mountain, uncles and aunts who are pelicans, crows and pigeons. Mother sea and grandfather winter and all the other cousins of fur and fin, feather, fern, thunder and harsh summer nights. It took growing up. Responsibility for being witch.

Do we need another 101? To add to the plethora of variations of the same? No.

WITCH consists of contemplations and lore for a grimoire. Anarchism. Lore for today. Celtic myths retold, because I am indigenous to northern and arctic lands and have no right to misappropriate the culture of others. But… the penned myths and stories gathered from a non-literate ancestry, and so often suggested we learn from authorities or academics, scholars of such, heads of magical orders of one denomination or another, were written up by monks, long-indoctrinated, therefore how much credence should we allow?

The first essay, *The Lost Language of Story*, might, by the strictures of rapacious religion, be the most difficult, so you can leave it till last if you choose. It should make more sense then and begin, for us, a revolution of non-clichéd witch stories. Your own. Your lover's. Your children's. The people you truly learned from.

This grimoire suggests witches lose the pointy hat problem, the broomstick, the long black velvet cloak (unless it's your daily apparel), the trapping that seek to lure any one of us into not *being*, and *doing*, but into *needing* acknowledgment. We should be demanding authenticity from each other. From those who claim authority. Sure, we all wear our colors. Of course. But it's also necessary, at some stage, to admit that the pentagram is the path of the planet named *Venus*, as observed from Earth. Venus orbits the sun approximately thirteen times, for every eight orbits of us, and the tips of the five loops at the center of this magnificent geometric figure have the same relationship to one another as the five points of a pentagram. The design is beautiful for that reason, not, as some say, as the symbol of *a* witch. It has been claimed. I experience no conundrum with that, but knowing its mystery is to not be thought loopy. I am so tired of that. Many people, also witch, are tired of this old story.

Witch is animist. Witch is also heretical in the true meaning of the word which is *the right to choose*. Anarchist, not in the common, modern misnomer of misrule, rioting and carnage but in the etymological sense of having no leadership. Witch moves like the wind in the treetops or the waves on the shore. We can change our minds, deepen and not be conibeared by rules. We will never be mainstream. All that consumption. All that carelessness. Is it caused by a deviant gene? A purposefully implanted blind spot in the brain? Some synapses that don't register the pain of our other species living in feed lots, or sow stalls, or penned in vivisection laboratories or hunted for trophy or selfies?

So many of you have written to me, had cups of tea with me in Sydney or Galway, conversed over lunch at the head of the Mississippi in Minnesota, on skype conversations from Canada, across vast oceans and sky, here in Melbourne. More happens tomorrow when students come and sit with me. Happened in New Zealand when the wild and feral Nelson mob met. In Arizona. On the Isle of Stenness, north of Scotland. Tasmania in the cold, dark days, at the mere prick of spring bud.

You've said *Where do we go now, what do we do now*, and many of you have fallen victim to cult-like money-grabbing coven groups who can teach you very little.

There are artistic and theatrical organizations popping up around the earth, gathering crowds for huge midwinter celebrations, to feast Samhain and Beltane, to meet kindred and to finally feel we have come somewhere, as a rewilded people who know the religions are false.

These stories and wanderings are collected and collated for you.

7. INTRODUCTION
13. CONTENTS
15. PLEASE READ THE PREAMBLE FIRST:: *WHAT IS A GOD?*

18. The Lost Language of Story

85. Midwinter Solstice

99. When you Love Somebody

102. Spring Equinox

119. A Selkie Love Story

123. Midsummer Solstice

139. Forest People

147. What Would Happen if Everybody Started Telling the Truth?

181. Autumn Equinox

194. Seeing in the Dark: A Lost Soul Story

208. Paleface

213. Sometimes There are Reasons for Being Anonymous and Lost

219. How God Kills the World

235. The History of Snow

245. Rewilding Christmas

247. An Old Stone House with a Warped Slate Roof

251. Interview with America

265. A Mind Like Clear Water

269. Beltane is Not Halloween

275. The First Forest

281. I Have Touched You – On Love and the Wild God

283. Author's Note

287. About Ly de Angeles

PREAMBLE/MUST READ

WHAT IS A GOD?

JUST SO WE'RE CLEAR, WHEN THE word pops up anywhere in the following stories, god is not a person. God is not a name, and god is not *a* god, as we have been brainwashed to think of a god. Gods have no genders and they are not an *it*. They're us.

Just so you know, if I use the word god, I don't infer a deity. Because I have no religion. I do not worship. We are belonging. In the way of present-continuous. God is the whole, being the sum of its parts, but not greater than them. God is the land you are, and have been since before you were recognizably human, and that of your ancestors of every species, of every flora, of every river, each wave upon the sand of an atoll. Each susurration that laps the shingles of a Cornish beach. The macaw within a Brazilian rainforest canopy. The blue fungus that teaches the dreamer sight. What you know of them. That they know you. The names of plants, and the plants that are unknown and unnamed. That you are them, long after your body has ceased to be the *you* that people perceive you to be now. Or even that *you* think you are.

Gods are lovers and wildfires and volcanic eruptions. They are as plentiful and as rare as secrets, labyrinths and gargoyles. I think Neil Gaimon's *American Gods* comes closest. The premise of that story is that migrating people bring the old gods of the old lands with them, and very often, over generations, those people forget. These gods are then up to whatever tricks they choose, to remain significant. Even simply among themselves.

A god can be a certain rock, along the Birdsville Track in Australia, when there was no Birdsville Track. That rock is a wayshower. Its name is sung and danced and painted by indigenous people who know that to pass it by, and head north at a certain time of year, will lead them (and with the guidance of many other such gods) to the trading bay with the people who travel the sea routes (also gods) from elsewhere, for that trade. They are every Tarkine old-growth forest, every Huron lake and every Eyjafjallajökull volcano

So now we have established what I intend, should I use the god word anywhere in this (or any other book). When a tall, dark-skinned man named Hunter, introduces himself as a forest god, he doesn't necessarily say which forest. And he only appears to be a *he*. He is everything in the forest and, as such, could be any forest. At any time. Could also be the forest long since devastated for logging. Forgotten except as myth: a story with no known author.

As you work your way through this lore, this gathering of teachings, this story-telling of ravens, please spare a thought for the effect any of us have on a god, or the gods, if we grade a road and remove that stone on the Birdsville Track, bulldoze a forest (a god) and cover the earth (a god) with concrete, build a dam where a free river (a god) once thundered, construct a city, desecrate the bones of ancestral dead, of any species, terrorize the penned herds (gods) that are descended from what once were seasonally migrating aurochs. Spare a thought pertaining to our ignorance at treading roughshod over what has lived for a quaintly estimated 4.5 billion years. That makes us, also gods, yes? What kind of gods are we? What kind of god communes with me?

Just for a moment, let us consider this because, in the time of the era of the sixth mass extinctions, those we are destroying are also gods. And their silence is deafening.

When I meet a wild god, it is as likely to be the bricks in the wall that were once the clays along the riverbed. The true magic of witch is to listen. To everything. To be the grains of sand that are the gods of future atolls, holding stories within their warmth for when the next Ice Age sets us free to remember.

THE LOST LANGUAGE OF STORY

Animism and the Method of Loci

(An anthem to the Brave)

eleuthromania
(n.) an intense and irresistible
desire for freedom

Ringa ringa roses,
Pocket full of posies
A'tissue a'tissue,
We all fall down

I'M QUITE CERTAIN WE KNOW WHAT THE problems with people are. Something is missing. Even if we're living with a large gaggle of family. Even if we work in a crowded factory. Even if we are surrounded by senators or CEOs. Makes no difference. There's this deep well of knowing, that all that is familiar could disappear in an instant. That we're going to die. Likely within the next ten minutes to eighty years. What happens after that? What happens before we are born? Where are we? Deep, deep down the dark, rickety, rarely trod steps, in the little, locked room at the very end of consciousness, we wonder if anybody honestly and truly knows.

What if there's no *afterlife*? No tunnel with white light at the end? No heaven? No hell? Reincarnation is some old story just to make us feel okay about anybody, including us, dying? We just get laid in a coffin, are buried in a line of other coffins in a cemetery, that probably won't last a hundred years before it is dug up and the bones all secretly discarded? If we're merely *thinking meat*? That this body is all I am?

What happens if there is no purpose to life at all? Not ever? That within two hundred years nobody will know we ever existed? That we have lived, only to be eternally forgotten? No other animal remembers, do they?

Or *do* they? Are there ways of knowing exactly what happens to us? The answer is yes.

PART 1

You better lose yourself in the music, the moment
You own it, you better never let it go
You only get one shot, do not miss your chance to blow
This opportunity comes once in a lifetime[1]

WHAT ARE WE?

LONG, LONG AGO, SCIENCE WRITES, A singularity happened that produced a Big Bang[2]. And all the stars were born. All that would ever comprise the known universe entered into existence. The super explosion that also gave birth to time.

Several billion years later, after differentiating from everyone else in the universe, here we are. Earth. And currently, we are a sea of hominidae of every color and garment, with vastly differing cultures, rites, laws, beliefs and myths, our bodies being 90% bacteria.

If I internally invoke images of us as a species now, I see a sea of upturned faces. I see crowds suffering starvation and desperation, because of some environmental or human disaster. Because of war or religion. Killing over land rights or water rights and an endless fight against colonial usurpation and, by those who seek to reap the benefits *of* colonial domination and misrule, thinly disguised as authority.

I imagine women washing saris in the waters of the Ganges.

---

[1] Eminem, *Lose Yourself*
[2] http://www.hawking.org.uk/the-beginning-of-time.html

Massai warriors bleeding cattle. Yolngu people dancing in the red dust of the earth of the Dhuwa and Yirritja[3].

On Bourke Street, in Melbourne I see the opposite. I see a mass of downturned faces, every one of them in some unholy communion with a mobile device. And I ask myself, who are we? Because we, and all the above, *seem* to be strangers. We're not.

The same iron that has hurtled ceaselessly throughout the cosmos since the Big Bang forms our hemoglobin. The hydrogen that forms stars also powers the mitochondria in each cells of an animal body. Add oxygen to the mix and that is us, as water. Where did we come from? We always are. Every one of us is the universe, and when—even if—we die, we don't go away. There is nowhere to go because everywhere is here.

Suppose, these years of a twenty first century, according to the Gregorian calendar (which is, by the way, ludicrous), the 7,573,581,986 and counting people alive today, all die at once? Where will we go? And, if we all die at once, all the theories cease with us. So, what happens? Not the following, but let's address it first:

AFTERLIFE

---

[3] http://www.dhimurru.com.au/yolngu-culture.html

Christian theology supports of the concepts of heaven, hell, purgatory and limbo. These ideas are not new and certainly not exclusive to that religion. The mythology predates christianity by several thousand years, its origin, as far as we can ascertain, Mesopotamian. Variations of the same theme, some very intricate and complex, are found with the buddhist *Shambhala*, judaic *Olam Haba* and islamic *Jannah* or *Jahannam*.

The themes of happy heaven and horrifying hell, all seem rooted in Zoroastrianism, credited as being the first account of a dogmatic religion in recorded history. Dating is uncertain as there is no scholarly consensus, but on linguistic and socio-cultural evidence Zoroaster is assumed at somewhere between the first and second millennium BCE.

ZOROASTRIAN AFTERLIFE – *HEAVEN*

The soul of a dead person was said to hang about its body for three days, before entering a between-world where it must cross a river, be met with three entities who are judges, and who join the soul in crossing a bridge into the afterlife, the destination being either a *heaven* or a *hell*.

This, from the *Dadestin-i Denig*[4] that it is *lofty, exalted, and supreme, most brilliant, most fragrant, and most pure, most supplied with beautiful existences, most desirable, and most good, and the place and abode of the sacred beings. And in it are all comfort, pleasure, joy, happiness, and welfare, more and better even than the greatest and most supreme welfare and pleasure in the world; and there is no want, pain, distress, or discomfort whatever in it; and its pleasantness and: the welfare of the angels, is from that constantly beneficial place, the full and undiminishable space, the good and boundless world. And the freedom of the heavenly from danger from evil in heaven is like unto their freedom from disturbance, and the coming of the good angel is like unto the heavenly ones' own good works*

provided. This prosperity and welfare of the spiritual existence is more than that of the world, as much as that which is unlimited and everlasting, is more than that which is limited and demoniacal."

ZOROASTRIAN AFTERLIFE – *HELL*

---

[4] http://www.avesta.org/mp/dd.htm

Indeed, they may also be forced to ingest and devour horrid things (their own corpses, flesh and excrement, menstrual fluids and semen, blood and brains from skulls of the dead and their own children). Other punishments may be even more gruesome, including hanging (particularly upside-down), dismemberment, decapitation, laceration, mutilation and self-mutilation by cutting, gnawing, devouring, gnashing, piercing, beating, tearing, trampling, stinging and dragging. The wicked are stabbed and pelted, and stretched on racks; they are forced to bear enormous burdens, perform painful and fruitless tasks; are burned and cooked in ovens, cauldrons and frying-pans; are cast down into heat, cold and smoke, snow and stench.

They endure hunger and thirst; and they are forced to lick hot things or to defecate and masturbate continually; they are submerged in mud and turned into serpents; and, also, oddly bombarded with hedgehogs (a small spiny animal, native to Iran and popular as a pet among ancient Zoroastrians). In particular., the sense organs of the wicked are attacked: their eyes gouged out and their tongues pulled out; putrid substances are forced into their noses, eyes and mouths. Their sexual organs are also assaulted: their penises are gnawed, and their breasts are gnashed, and cut off.[5]"

STILL ON HELL

---

[5] http://www.hell-on-line.org/AboutZOR.html

With thoughts focused on the hereafter, Pope John Paul II expounded on heaven, hell and purgatory in his recent weekly audiences. The pope's messages reached the headlines of major newspapers as he denied heaven and hell were physical places and seemed to reverse nearly 2,000 years of christian teaching… The pope's denial of the traditional christian understanding of hell is one more step in a progressive rejection of the very real and very horrible picture of hell revealed in the Bible. The temptation to "air-condition hell," as one Roman catholic magazine put it, is constant in a secular world that rejects hell as outdated and promiseing some kind of vague harmonic convergence in the afterlife.[6]

ISLAMIC AFTERLIFE – *HEAVEN*

In the Quran, *The Garden* is described with material delights, such as beautiful maidens, precious stones, delicious foods, and constantly flowing water—the latter especially appealing to the desert dwelling Arabs, who spend most of their life in arid lands. Islamic texts describe immortal life as: one that is happy, without hurt, sorrow, fear or shame. Where every wish is fulfilled. Everyone will be thirty-three years old, and of the same status. The afterlife in paradise is one of bliss, including sumptuous robes as garments, jewelry and perfumes, exquisite banquets, served in priceless vessels by immortal youths, as the heavenly inhabitants recline on couches inlaid with gold and precious stones. Everything one longs for.

ISLAMIC AFTERLIFE – *HELL*

---

[6] http://www.albertmohler.com/2009/07/16/should-we-lose-the-fear-of-hell-the-pope-redefines-the-doctrine/

One collection of Quranic descriptions of hell include rather specific indications of the tortures of the fire, flames that crackle and roar, fierce, boiling waters, scorching winds and black smoke roaring as if it would burst with rage. Its wretched inhabitants sighing and wailing, their scorched skins constantly exchanged for new ones so that they can taste the torment afresh, food that is full of thorns and that fails to relieve hunger. The damned drink festering water, and though death appears on all sides. No one can escape. They are linked together in chains of 70 cubits, wear pitch for clothing and have fire on their faces. Boiling water is poured over their heads, melting their insides as well as their skins, and hooks of iron drag them back should they try to escape. Their remorseful admissions of wrongdoing and pleadings for forgiveness are in vain.

CHRISTIAN AFTERLIFE – *HEAVEN*

It is considered an actual *place*. Also called *Paradise*, the concept of which is so distorted in modern christianity, by sect, that a clear definition in so short a story as this is almost laughable. It is said to be *on high*, in the sky. Clouds are usually rendered white, with fluffy-winged, harp-playing angels reclining thereon. A man named *God* is there. Oh, and he also made *it* and everything else (including hell I suppose, since he's *omnipotent*). Except when there's a hurricane or a volcanic eruption. He's then either absurdly displeased with his people, and laying waste to them and their lives, but including every grass, flower, bark and herb, person of wing, fur, web, or other cousin that gets caught up in the event. Punishment. He encourages his people to wage war on Mother Nature. He is exceedingly old, but not decrepit, flaunts a flowing white beard and is the epitome of a patriarch. European features (quite like one would imagine the face of Aristotle), and a stern frown. His throne is gold, of course and his personally-agreed-to tortured only son sits beside him. It's a happy place where the soul exists in forever, basking in the old man's countenance. The rarer viewpoint is an Eden-like landscape where food and purity, meekness and all things of beauty will nourish a soul for, again, all eternity. What I don't know is if that is before or after the Second Coming of his son (see *Rapture*).

Case in point: not according to a Time Magazine interview [7] with Tom Wright, Bishop of Durham, considered the fourth most senior cleric in the church of England and author of *The Resurrection of the Son of God*. He argues forcefully for a literal interpretation of this event.

TIME MAGAZINE: But it's not where the real action is, so to speak?

WRIGHT: No. Our culture is very interested in life after death, but the New Testament is much more interested in what I've called the life *after* life after death — in the ultimate resurrection into the new heavens and the new Earth. Jesus' resurrection marks the beginning of a restoration that he will complete upon his return. Part of this will be the resurrection of all the dead, who will "awake," be embodied and

---

[7] http://content.time.com/time/world/article/0,8599,1710844,00.html

participate in the renewal. John Polkinghorne, a physicist and a priest, has put it this way:

God will download our software onto his hardware until the time he gives us new hardware to run the software again for ourselves." That gets to two things nicely: that the period after death is a period when we are in God's presence but not active in our own bodies, and also that the more important transformation will be when we are again embodied and administering Christ's kingdom.

It's called the *Rapture*:

"The meaning or definition of Rapture is the idea that the coming of Jesus will take place in two separate stages. The first will be a secret Rapture – or carrying away of the saved to heaven – at the beginning of a seven-year period of tribulation, during which the antichrist will appear. The second phase occurs at the close of the time of tribulation when Jesus will return to Earth in triumph and glory. At the Rapture, the Lord will descend bodily in the air for his saints, both for the dead and for the living (1 Thessalonians 4:16-17) which will be seven years prior to the Revelation of the second stage of His coming. In the first stage of the Rapture, the Lord comes for His church; whereas, at the end of the tribulation period, He comes back with His church. At this event "every eye shall see Him.[8]

Which is why christians inter corpses. The thought is intolerable

---

[8] http://www.beliefnet.com/faiths/christianity/6-things-every-christian-should-know-about-the-rapture.aspx?p=2

that they won't be the same person forever. Is this the foundation of the zombie? Resurrected before their time? I do suggest Wade Davis' book *The Serpent and the Rainbow* for an exhaustive understanding of Haitian zombifiction. But it must also be remembered that slavery in Haiti was brutally governed by the French who were christian. So, entombment, combined the spirit's return to Guinea (as an afterlife destination) with that of the christian version of an afterlife, is perchance a hybrid confusion.

CHRISTIAN AFTERLIFE – *HELL*

There are so many cults to this religion that the topic ranges from that of Zoroaster, to that of Islam. Amongst pentecostalists it's one thing, amongst baptists and catholics another. I tend to enjoy the following:

"Annihilationism theory doesn't fare much better in this regard. Threatening to kill me as opposed to threatening to set me on fire for ever and ever… You be the judge. But being wiped from existence is far different from being set on fire and tormented forever and ever and ever and ever and ever, time without end. That's beyond barbaric. We wouldn't set Hitler on fire for five minutes. But they worship someone who would set John Lennon on fire forever. That's sick, dudes.[9]

---

[9] https://twocultsurvivor.com/2016/02/23/the-threat-of-hell-is-pure-extortion/

THE AFTERLIFE OF OTHERS

THE ROMAN AND GREEK AFTERLIFE – *ELYSIAN FIELDS*
(According to Hesiod and Homer)

Hesiod lived at about the same time as Homer (8th or 7th century BCE). In Hesiod's *Works and Days*[10], he wrote of the deserving dead that:

"Father Zeus the son of Kronos gave a living and an abode apart from men and made them dwell at the ends of the earth. And they live untouched by sorrow in the Islands of the Blessed along the shore of deep swirling Okeanos (Oceanus), happy heroes for whom the grain-giving earth bears honey-sweet fruit flourishing thrice a year, far from the deathless gods, and Kronos rules over them; for the father of men and gods released him from his bonds. And these last equally have honor and glory."

According to Homer in his epic poems written around the 8th century BCE, Elysian Fields or Elysium refers to a beautiful meadow in the Underworld where the favored of Zeus enjoy perfect happiness. This was the ultimate paradise a hero could achieve: basically, an ancient Greek Heaven. In the *Odyssey*, Homer tells us that, in Elysium:

"Men lead an easier life than anywhere else in the world, for in Elysium here falls not rain, nor hail, nor snow, but Oceanus [the giant body of water surrounding the entire world] breathes ever with a West wind that sings softly from the sea, and gives fresh life to all men."

---

[10] https://people.sc.fsu.edu/~dduke/lectures/hesiod1.pdf

ROMAN AND GREEK AFTERLIFE – *IS THERE A HELL?*

According to several sources it's much more complicated than the christian kind, I suppose because they were a polytheistic people, so it had to be.

After a person's body dies, their essence (called a soul. And what *is* a soul? I assume it's a doppelganger of the invisible kind because to all extents and ensuing purposes it is the dead person but in an undead way) continues an existence.

"Upon death, a soul was led by Hermes near the entrance of the underworld, where the ferry awaited to carry it across to Acheron. There was a single ferry run by Charon, the boatman, who took the souls across the river. Only those who could pay the fare with coins placed on their lips or eyelids after death were granted passage; the rest were trapped between two worlds. After the boat ride, the souls entered through the gates; Cerebus allowed everyone to enter, but none to leave. The souls then appeared before a panel of three judges, Rhadamanthus, Minos, and Aeacus, who passed sentence based on their deeds during their previous life. The souls who were good went to the Elysian Fields, while the others were singled out for special treatment; Sisyphus and Tantalus are two examples of souls that were sentenced to be tormented for eternity.[11]"

One ferry? *One?* That's a real quote.

Elsewhere I read that six rivers link the real world to the *Underworld* and

---

[11] http://greekmythology.wikia.com/wiki/The_Underworld

on one threshold of the entrance are: Grief, Anxiety, Diseases, Old Age. Fear, Hunger, Death, Agony and Sleep, together with Guilty Joys. On the opposite threshold is War.

Charon is the name of *the* ferryman. He features alternatively as indistinct or ugly, filthy and grim. (I'm not surprised, considering the workload). Pay him one of two pennies and you're across (the other is if you get to come back because yes, for some there is rebirth. On the other side of the river are the aforementioned judges and off you go to either *Tartarus*, a pitch-black land of darkness described as being as far beneath the underworld as the earth is beneath the sky.

The wrongs that send you here are not mentioned. Then there's the *Asphodel Meadows*, a place for ordinary or indifferent souls who did not commit any significant crimes, but who also did not achieve any greatness or recognition and, of course, the *Mourning Fields*, a part of the underworld reserved for those who wasted their lives for unrequited love.

When I seek comprehension of the *what* or *where* of this *Underworld* is:

"The Underworld was hidden deep in the earth and was the kingdom of the dead, ruled by Hades, a greedy god whose sole purpose was to increase the number of souls in his kingdom; at the same time, very reluctant to let any soul leave. The Erinnyes[12] were welcomed in the Underworld. For most souls, life in the underworld was not particularly unpleasant. It was rather like being in a miserable dream,

---

[12] The *erinyes* were thought of as "three goddesses", seeking vengeance against anyone who had sworn a false oath or had done an evil act.

full of shadows, ill-lit and desolate, barren of hope; a joyless place where the dead slowly faded into nothingness.[13]"

I presume, by the way, because of the author's use of the past tense, this specific *Underworld* no longer exists.

SCANDINAVIAN/NORDIC AFTERLIFE – *VALHALLA*

Valhalla is the hall where the god Odin houses the dead whom he deems worthy of dwelling with him. The dead who reside in Valhalla, the *einherjar*, are warriors who die alone and who are brought to Valhalla by the *valkyries*[14]. The dead experience great pleasure: every day they fight and slaughter each other, enact feats of bravery or savagery, and every evening they are restored to full health. Their meat comes from *Saehrimnir* that some scholars consider a boar, others a sooty sea-beast that returns to life every time it is slaughtered and butchered. For their drink they have mead, fermented from the milk of the udder of *Heidrun* the goat, said to graze upon the *Læraðr* tree, also thought to be *Yggdrasil*, the Tree of Life (what could in Australia be equated with the indigenous idea of the Dreamtime).

The *einherjar* enjoy a copious supply of exquisite food and drink, yes, but they won't live this so-charmed experience eternally. Valhalla's battle-honed warriors are chosen by Odin who, in the perennial company of wolves and ravens, riding an eight-legged beast across the

---

[13]https://www.greekmythology.com/Myths/Places/The_Underworld/the_underworld.html
[14] Valkyries are a host of female figures who choose those who may die in battle and those who may live.

landscape (eight gathering times such as solstice and equinox, and the four main seasonal transitions recognized right across Celtic peoples, myths and lore), collects them for the purpose of having them come to his aid in his fated struggle against the wolf *Fenrir*, during *Ragnarök*[15] – a battle in which Odin and these undead warriors are doomed, forever this time, to annihilation.

The most famous description of Valhalla in Old Norse literature that of *Grímnismál*[16], portrays it as located in *Asgard*: sky. However, other lines of evidence suggest that it was at least sometimes underground, like the more general underworld. As we've noted above, the continual battle that takes place in Valhalla is one of the place's defining features.

---

[15] Ragnarök is a series of future events, including a great battle, foretold to ultimately result in the death of a number of major figures (including the gods Odin, Thor, Týr, Freyr, Heimdallr and Loki), the occurrence of various natural disasters, and the subsequent submersion of the world in water. Afterward, the world will resurface anew and fertile, the surviving and returning gods will meet, and the world will be repopulated by two human survivors.

[16] http://www.sacred-texts.com/neu/poe/poe06.htm

THE FOLLOWING IS RELEVANT IN PART 2 (REMEMBERING):

Icelandic people retained their pre-christian lore perhaps deeply into the current era. Some retain it still. The oral literatures of Iceland, anonymous—ergo mythic poetry, *The Poetic Edda*—were not committed to paper until between 1000 and 1300 CE by now-christianised scholars and monks. Further tainting would have occurred with English translations.

"Like most early poetry, the *Eddic* poems were minstrel poems, passing orally from singer to singer and from poet to poet for centuries. None of the poems are attributed to a specific author, though many of them show strong individual characteristics and are likely to have been the work of individual poets. Scholars sometimes speculate on hypothetical authors, but firm and accepted conclusions have never been reached."[17]

"2. I remember yet | the giants of yore,
Who gave me bread | in the days gone by;
Nine worlds I knew, | the nine in the tree
With mighty roots | beneath the mold."[18]

Of all the texts available this is quite clearly in the style of poetic mnemonics; the holding of lore and ancestry being told orally in the style of *Mary had a little lamb | its fleece was white as snow…*

---

[17] https://en.wikipedia.org/wiki/Poetic_Edda
[18] The full translation, The Poetic Edda, was compiled by Henry Adams Bellows in 1936 and is available online.

This is epic seasonal and ancestral lore. Other Occidental and Oriental Otherworld stories will have the same at their root, but I leave you to hunt them. For now, I ask only that you read the words and recognize the repetition of certain words, titles and terminology to comprehend how relentless the misinformation and brainwashing has become.

EGYPTIAN AFTERLIFE – *FIELD OF RUSHES*

The *Field of Rushes* is the afterlife world of the ancient Egyptians – a *paradise* that people worked their entire lives towards. To the underworld. Throughout the underworld journey, the dead person's soul must contend with gods, strange creatures and gatekeepers to reach Osiris and the Hall of Final Judgment. Here they plead their case for entry into the afterlife. Once the journey through the underworld is complete, the soul reaches the Hall of Final Judgment where processing involves two-parts:

Firstly, the soul stands before forty-two divine judges[19] and plead their innocence of any wrongdoing during their lifetime. The *Book of the Dead* provides them with the correct words to use for each of the judges, ascertaining that they will pass the test of this process even if they have not been completely fault-free.

The second process is the weighing of the heart (yes, a soul has a heart): the heart is said to contain a record of all the person's actions while alive. It is weighed against a feather on the scales of a feminized

---

[19] https://www.ancient.eu/article/185/the-forty-two-judges/

deity named *Ma'at*. This feather is the symbol of truth and determines whether the soul is honest or not. If the heart is heavier than the feather, it is fed to *Ammut the Devourer*, and the soul is cast into darkness. If the scales are balanced, the soul has passed the test and is brought before *Osiris* who welcomes it into the afterlife. For those who are concerned about this test, they can recite a spell (usually Spell 30B from the *Book of the Dead*) and inscribe it onto their heart scarab amulet to prevent its betrayal.

Life in the *Field of Rushes*, reflects the real world they have supposedly left behind, with blue skies, rivers and boats for travel, gods and goddesses to worship, and fields and crops that needed to be ploughed and harvested. The dead are granted a plot of land and are expected to maintain it, either by performing the labor themselves or getting their *shabtis* to work for them. *Shabtis* (small statuettes) are often supplied with agricultural tools such as baskets and hoes and are often led by a foreman or overseer (who appears after about 1000 BCE), who carries a flail instead of tools.

WELSH/BRITISH AFTERLIFE

There isn't one.

I'll repeat that: there isn't one.

The myth that *annwn* is an *Underworld*, seems to have been correlated post-christianity to give a hell that did not exist, just because the monks of the Middle Ages needed it to fit a pre-determined mould so obstinately. However, let's go there…

ANNWN

In Welsh mythology, Yr Annwn, is variously described as being The Fortunate Isles (in the western sea… strikingly similar to the Greek Blessed Isles, also in the Atlantic Ocean), actually underground, or just being with us but invisible, as if in another dimension. Gods and mortals could go there if they were shown how, invited, or tricked into going there… It is interesting to note that the Otherworld was not where you went when you died in original Celtic mythology, it was somewhere that co-existed with this world in parallel. The Christians put the spin on it that it was the Afterlife, to make it more compatible with their own beliefs. Annwn was just a place of permanent happiness and eternal youth.[20]

Except…

---

[20] http://fatetwister-waynegamm.com/annwn-the-otherworld.html

PART 2

Imagine there's no heaven,
It's easy if you try.
No hell below us,
Above us only sky…[21]

IMMRAM[22] AND THE UNDERWORLD

Immram are tales written about travels. They are considered just stories. Why? Also called myths but in such a way as to imply they are not real, when *myth* is the retelling of a story with no known author.

The following explanation is limited but serves to suffice: "Immrama [plural] meaning 'voyages' or literally 'rowings about' refers to a category of medieval Irish Christian literature in which a protagonist sets about voyaging in penance for sins committed. Medieval catalogues of literature see this genre as contrasting with *eachtra*[23], 'expeditions' or 'adventures' in which the protagonist visits the *Otherworld* or Irish traditional lore.[24]"

---

[21] John Lennon, *Plastic Ono Band*
[22] Pronounced IM/rav, emphasis on the first syllable, plural IM/rvuh
[23] Adventures, pronounced A/ktruh
[24] https://en.wikipedia.org/wiki/Imrama

There are two ways of experiencing an *immram*. It is written that people can reach further shores and experience other lands by entering ancient burial mounds or caves, or... by boat, crossing the sea.

So, there are two considerations here. Firstly, that of a hypnotic, ecstatic or spiritual experience and secondly that people did indeed travel: west, by sea, to what is now known as the Americas, including several islands that may have long-since been be drowned, or that could as easily be the Canary Islands, the Faroes, Azores or Madeira. This is not to imply that Europe, Siberia, Tibet and China were not also visited for trade, stories and heroic quests.

I'll return to the first instance in a moment, as it is important, but let us first look at real journeys. There is sufficient evidence for an Irish settlement in North Carolina, a people called the Duhare. Kerry O'Shea, of Irish Central (online) suggests (3rd hand but worthy of a follow-up): *It was found that Datha, the name of the leader of Duhare, was a standard Medieval Irish Gaelic word that means "painted." Datha of Duhare was remembered for being tattooed or painted as if to separate himself from the commoners – a tradition among Celts.*[25]

And further, *Researchers began to investigate the similarity of Irish rock carvings to those in the state of South Carolina. One member of the People of One Fire team came across an ancient Irish lullaby entitled "Bainne nam fiadh" – On milk of deer I was reared. On milk of deer I was nurtured. On milk of deer beneath the ridge of storms on crest of hill and mountain.*

---

[25] https://www.irishcentral.com/roots/history/old-spanish-document-suggests-irish-were-in-america-before-columbus-190817901-237769001

Another article writes: "In 1526, Spanish explorer Lucas Vazquez de Ayllon landed in modern-day South Carolina around the area of the Santee River. He visited with many of the Native American tribes in the area and recorded their customs, rituals, and ways of living. While visiting a province named Duhare he witnessed many unusual things. First, he noted that the people of this province were white not Native American. Second, he noted that the king of Duhare, named Datha, and his wife were much taller than the commoners and lived in a palace built of stone. He noted their hair was brown and hung to the ground.[26]"

---

[26] http://lostworlds.org/tag/duhare/

The idea of *immram* also states, in many texts, that a journey took place in a cave, a *sídhe*[27] (pronounced *she*) mound or a long barrow made intentionally for ceremonial purposes. These are prevalent in Ireland, such as Knowth, Dowth, Newgrange, and in England at West Kennett Long Barrow, Avesbury, Barrow Hill in Somerset, and in Alba (Scotland), at the Cairns of Camster at Cathness, while the Knowes of Trotty on Orkney has revealed a cache of gold and amber. Tiny fragments of bone indicate nothing thus far, as archaeologists have not been able to ascertain if they are human, leading to speculation that they could be those of other species. An *immram* in a cave, stone circle or especially-built tumuli would only have been conducted for mystical purposes, and most likely also occurred in the closed-system environments of specifically erected henges or stone circles, meant for secret, occult business and not for general gatherings of clan/s.

Were these underground or closed-system stone monuments graves? Certainly, the charred bones of cremated people have been unearthed within some. But very few. At Stonehenge a mere two hundred and forty bones have been found, over a fifteen-hundred-year period of consistent usage: "Almost everyone who died in Neolithic Britain left no trace.[28]"

Creating underground environments, or engaging in closed or specific rites or rituals in caves, is to be *within* Earth, a womb-like experience in which to dream: *Under the world*. It was never allegory.

---

[27] Sídhe pronounced *she*, is a hand-made mound within which is cave-like
[28] Lynne Kelly, The Memory Code, (p. 116)

The worldwide use of psychoactive plants, such as fly agaric, peyote, ayahuasca and silene undulata, and including henbane, datura, mandrake and acacia, have long been used for ecstatic learning purposes. They may have been ingested to train the apprentice or to advance the knowledge of healing species or ceremony, of recitation and memory enhancement. Why would it be different in Britain and Ireland to the rest of Europe or the Middle and Far East? From north to South America? Asia, Africa and the Caribbean?

Of his personal experience of magic mushrooms in Mexico in 1955 Robert Gordon Wasson[29] writes:

"We were never more wide awake, and the visions came whether our eyes were opened or closed. They emerged from the center of the field of vision, opening up as they came, now rushing, now slowly, at the pace that our will chose. They were in vivid colour, always harmonious. They began with art motifs, angular such as might decorate carpets or textiles or wallpaper or the drawing board of an

architect. Then they evolved into palaces with courts, arcades, gardens--resplendent palaces all laid over with semiprecious stones."

---

[29] https://en.wikipedia.org/wiki/R._Gordon_Wasson

And later: "In ancient Greece and Rome there was a belief that certain kinds of mushrooms were procreated by the lightning bolt. We made the further discovery that this particular myth, for which no support exists in natural science, is still believed among many widely scattered peoples: the Arabs of the desert, the peoples of India, Persia and the Pamirs, the Tibetans and Chinese, the Filipinos and the Maoris of New Zealand, and even among the Zapotecs of Mexico. This would explain the aura of the supernatural in which all fungi seem to be bathed. We were the first to offer the conjecture of a divine mushroom in the remote cultural background of the European peoples, and the conjecture at once posed a further problem: what kind of mushroom was once worshiped and why?[30]"

With the advance of Rome and the destruction of the druid Isle of Mona (Ynis Môn) much knowledge of the mystical use of psychoactive plants, in use as ceremonial *immrama*, would have passed into secrecy, to be taught orally over consecutive generation, into the christian era of advanced repression. Timothy Leary and many other scientists have confirmed the efficacy of these substances and even today the research into treating depression with micro-dosing psilocybin continues. Fly agaric has been decorating children's storybook covers since the Victorian era and is even depicted on a Russian stamp.

---

[30] Full article http://www.imaginaria.org/wasson/life.htm

All those *Afterlives*. Such detail. Surely, they can't be mere fantasies. Some guys sitting around all serious. One guy turns to the other and says, 'Hey, you know what we need to come up with to control the unwashed masses and get them to do what we say, don't you? We need to invent places for them to go after they die, man. And if we get all the rules right we've got meek people just turning the other cheek towards us when we slap them!' 'Gold!' Says the other guy. How can we make a buck out of it?'

If, as in the vast amount of detail in the biblical book of *Ezekiel* attests, I suspect they were tripping on *soma*, in a form of vision quest, in the days they were still tribal hunter gatherers (because the systems look to be in place at the time of the Agricultural Revolution). Or one of the chieftains dreamed the entire thing in the finest detail so that it was relegated to religious doctrine... *or* it's an animist understanding of the seasons of the tribe and the animist understandings of laws and ceremonial practice of which we know absolutely nothing.

STORY AND –*ACH* REVISITED

Underworld is written of by most as a real place, rather than a state of being, and variations are repeated on new-age sites, by certain schools of myth and by proponents of western mystery cults, without any explanation as to what is meant. The entirety of a people called the Tuatha Dé Dannan are said to have gone into the Underworld at their defeat by the Milesians, purported to be the modern Irish. Stories abound of magic cities and spears and cauldrons (Latin for *cooking pot* and not some magical vessel).

The stories of the heroic Cú Chullain (hound of the smith, Chullain), of how he went from being a boy named Sétanta to becoming said hound, his salmon leap across a bridge to the Isle of Skye where he learned to fight from a warrior woman named Scáth-ach and, of course, of *queen* Mebd[31] and the *Táin Bó Cúailnge* (Cattle Raid of Coolie). I know there are secrets in these. More shapeshifting (animism, totemism): more –achs to tell us what is.

The Cattle Raid of Coolie seems to be about two bulls and whose bull is better, but let's go deeply into the mythos before we reject outright just another vain power struggle over cattle by people. Because that may be how the monks wrote it, but it has, in the modern era been written as literal by far too many since.

---

[31] Mebh: pronounced mayve.

SIMPLIFYING THE STORY OF THE TÁIN BÓ CÚAILNGE

When using these sources, it is, as always, important to question the impact of the circumstances in which they were produced. Most of the manuscripts were created by Christian monks, who may well have been torn between the desire to record their native culture and their religious hostility to pagan beliefs resulting in some of the gods being euphemized. Many of the later sources may also have formed part of a propaganda effort designed to create a history for the people of Ireland that could bear comparison with the mythological descent of their British invaders from the founders of Rome that was promulgated by Geoffrey of Monmouth and others. There was also a tendency to rework Irish genealogies to fit into the known schema of Greek or Biblical genealogy.[32]

Mabh (sometimes Mebh) is *queen* of Connacht, the lush west coast of Ireland and abides at (or is) the enormous hill fort of Rathcroghan (*rath*, like *dun*, is another word for a fortress). She (it/they) is married (or something to that effect) to *Ailill* (which means *elf*, so that he/it may not have been a human) although she had several other *husbands* (or consorts) beforehand. She *owns* the most fertile bull in the world but, according to the story, the bull, named *Finnbhenn-ach* (white horn), scorns being in the possession of a woman and joins *Ailill's* herd. *Ailill* is now wealthier than *Mabh* (remember cattle were the currency of the Irish for millennia). She (it/they) decides to acquire an even more fertile bull named *Donn Cuailnge*, the Brown Bull of Coolie. He is owned (for lack of a better word) by *Dáire mac Fiachna*, said to be a

---

[32] https://en.wikipedia.org/wiki/Irish_mythology

cattle lord (or tribe) of Ulster up along the northeast coast. What's worthy of remembering, here, is that *mac Fiachna is from the family of* and *Fiachna*, from what I have dug up from the antiquarian soil may well have been a confederacy of Cruitne tribes, the Dál nAraidi, neighbours of the Dál Riata just across the narrow sea to what is now the far east coast of Scotland.

The name, or title, *Mabh* is thought to be mead, and in ancient and medieval Ireland the drinking of mead was a key part of a *king's* inauguration ceremony, considered a delicacy. I even go so far as to suggest *Mabd* was *only* mead, anthropomorphized in myth as a woman.

Mabd makes a deal with *Dáire* to borrow *Donn Cuailnge* for a year after offering him (them) both wealth and herself. He accepts.

Some Fool (they are necessary to a story, similar or same as a trickster) gets drunk on said mead and fabricates a boast that *Mabh* would have taken the bull by force if *Dáire* had not agreed to her terms. *Dáire* believes the Fool and reneges on the deal.

Mabh wages war because war is always fought because someone wants something not theirs out of greed or vanity. If war it was… Or are we just repeating a word that may mean something else? A question of vital importance.

The warriors of Ulster fall ill under what is thought to be the curse of *Macha* (sovereign land of Ulster) caused by disrespecting women in pregnancy by making them perform feats they are not fit for. The curse is weakness and is written to have been laid on her *husband*.

This curse was intended to affect the men of Ulster for a nine day period (Celtic lore has nine elements called the *duíle* (pronounced doolie) and in this story it *seemingly* lasts for months.

I suggest *seemingly* (although I do not think the Celtic view of anything is linear) because, as I have already mentioned, many stories that seem to fit a timeline are most likely referring to annual or even generational events.

So, to help in their defense the cursed warriors (or warrior class/clan) call on seventeen-year old champion and shape-shifter *Cú Chullain*.

Before I get to an eventual involvement between *Cú Chullain* and the *Mórrigan*, there is a strange aspect to the tale. Some texts I've read maintain that Cú Chullain and a few of his buddies snuck up on the Brown Bull and stole him without being found out. That the fight started after that. Then there's the story of his fellow warrior *Cethern mac Fintain*, a 'man' with silver hair and a silver spear, who rode his chariot into battle and, although killing many of what I assume were the Connachta, is said to have received severe wounds. But, there is something not quite right in the following account: When he is wounded, the Ulster forces rescue him. He kills healers (fifteen or as many as fifty) who attempt to treat him because he does not like their unfavorable diagnoses. The other Ulstermen listen patiently when he explains how he acquired his many wounds, one of which was delivered by *Medb*.

Cú Chullain finally restores *Cethern's* health with bone marrow and animal ribs and the latter then returns to battle, killing Connachta again, before he himself falls.

Lost yet?

Why would *Cethern* kill those healers? If he (it/they) killed one, why would forty nine others take his/her place? How could someone tell of what each individual wound meant? And that one was dealt by *Mabh*? Something is missing. *Cethern* (whose father is Fintan mac Néill) is also a teacher of *Fionn mac Cumhaill*, in the *Fenian Cycle*.

What does he teach?

For thousands of years silver has been used as a healing and anti-bacterial agent by civilizations throughout the world. Its medical, preservative and restorative powers can be traced as far back as the ancient Greek and Roman Empires. Long before the development of modern pharmaceuticals, silver was employed as a germicide and antibiotic.[33]

The above quote includes druidic use as well as ayurvedic healing practice and lore. Why not? Are we missing a key point here? Is this section an allegorical teaching mnemonic? Only when the final healer could explain the source of each individual wound could a choice of life or death be made. By the *teacher*, not the healer.

The name Fintan/Fintain is still in use Ireland in the 1800s. I wrote briefly of the burial of James Fintan Lalor, brother of Peter Lalor ex Eureka Uprising fame, in a novella titled *Bakery Hill*[34], published 2017. James, or rightly Séamas Fionntán Ó Leathlobhair was an Irish revolutionary, journalist, and one of the most influential writers of his day. A leading member of the Irish Confederation (Young Ireland), he

---

[33] http://www.silver-colloids.com/Pubs/history-silver.html
[34] https://www.academia.edu/34919664/Bakery_Hill_-_a_Novella_2017.doc

was to play an active part in both the Rebellion in July 1848 and the attempted Rising in September of that same year. He was arrested. The illness he contracted in prison killed him.

Why is this relevant? Padraig Lalor, his father, calls the family one of the seven septs of Ireland (County Laois) and claims to be descended from the Red Branch royal house of Ulster. That would signify that Cethern, teacher of Fionn mac Cumhaill and ally of Cú Chullain is an ancestor of Peter Fintan Lalor.

Whether this is an actuality or not, why give (at least) two brothers in the same family the same middle name? In genealogy it is often the custom, in Wales, Scotland and Ireland to add the name of an ancestral branch before the surname. My genealogist friend has the Welsh middle name that is nestled in the mists of many hundred years. That name is a crossroads, a woman of consequence who joined a lineage through *marriage*. Retention continues the story. I also think it significant that 'royal' genealogies have always been kept, and yet the practice is never encouraged amongst those considered by peerage as irrelevant. Like you and me.

Back to the story...

Before one specific combat *Cú Chullain* is written to meet the *Mórrigan*. Said to be a *deity* (vernacular: goddess) but is not. This is a *god*. Genius-loci specific to a region. Two words *mór*: Huge or large, *rí*: queen, but *is* the landscape of Rathcroghan (the hill fort region of Connacht).

She visits *Cú Chullain* in the form of a beautiful young woman and offers him her love, but he rejects her. She then reveals herself and threatens to interfere in his next fight. She first becomes an eel that trips him in the river, then a wolf that stampedes cattle, and finally the heifer at the head of that stampede. But *Cú Chullain* wounds her each time. After these defeats the *Mórrigan* appears to him in the form of an old woman milking a cow, with wounds corresponding to the ones *Cú Chullain* gave her in her animal forms. She offers him three drinks of milk. With each drink he blesses her, and the blessings heal her wounds.

This requires deconstruction:

- *Cú Chullain* has been recruited by the Ulster chieftain *Dáire mac Fiachna* because his own warriors are still under the sickness/curse.
- *Cú Chullain* and his buddy *Cethern mac Fintain* go on the warpath against the warriors of *Mabh*.
- She sends these out to fight him one by one so there is only ever single combat.

None of this rings true. I think we could be looking at a lineage because *Mabh* is not a woman. She *is* Rathcroghan just as *Mórrigan* is one of two places: either also the entire territory of Connacht or Inis Mór off the coast. As within the story is the reference to head or headland. And Inis Mór is the genius loci facing out to the western sea/sunset where *Llugh*, who turns up at the scene to heal *Cú Chullain* (claiming him as his son) is the actual sun itself, not a person. *Llugh* is also said to be storms and sky.

Llugh puts *Cú Chullain* to sleep for three days (the number three is a recurring theme in Celtic literature, said to be earth, sky and sea. Deeply within this is the understanding of the seasonal festival of Samhain, in preparation for the long dark, which is the time of the seeds beneath the snow, that are the children/food of tomorrow, that will sustain the people (human and other species) from the coming spring onwards, indefinitely.

While we're in myth world it is worth remembering that human representatives of a clan or region were often considered *wedded* to the landscape. We cannot just say *land* because that invokes a limited image into consciousness, of fields and meadows. Landscape includes weather, species, plant, river, springs, mountain, ocean and naming. Also, women and men were not classed as better than, or less important, than each other. The monks who scribed these stories were well under the thrall of the church of Rome by the 11th and 12th centuries when these accounts were written. Unfortunately, the *Chinese Whisper* effect would have been responsible for the appearance of a dominant patriarchal to taint hitherto non-literate, oral and ancestral accounts.

This *wedding* to the land of a chieftain, no matter the gender, requires attention to some obscure stories that can, again, seem like throwaway statements. Mabh's current husband is Ailill[35]. This name is written to have three meanings: elf, king of the fair folk[36] (or sídhe) and stone. The story of the *Táin Bó Cúailnge* introduces us to an indigenous and inclusive lore. By the time the pages of fallible history were written up by the monks the invasions of Celtic Britain and Ireland were almost complete. The Normans were yet to come but the influence of the Norse was already interwoven with the landscape of the times. The word *elf* is a Saxon/Scandinavian word meaning *white being*. It also translates across to both *Alba* and *Albion* (Scotland) With animacy that would represent many things: snow, frost, ice, mist, the light on the horizon of the ocean at dawn, the blossoms of the apple tree in spring, ice, glacier, cloud not carrying rain, starlight. County Galway's coastline is particularly interesting as the rock is called *metamorphic,* a form of quartz. The rock is striated with white.

"Gems and precious stones are some examples of metamorphic rocks. These stones are found deep underground or inside mountains.[37]"

A point to consider is that the Irish were great seafarers and even the legend of the *kelpie* relates to the white backward-spraying foam of waves heaving both forward and backward in strong storm or fierce wind, appearing like the long manes of white horses at full gallop.

---

[35] https://www.mybabynames.net/name/Ailill
[36] And that is a whole other can of worms
[37] https://www.reference.com/science/can-metamorphic-rocks-found-3dd4f3f23f019b44

In the instance of *Mabh* being married to *Ailill* then, we could also consider her to be a chieftain *wedded* to the entire landscape, generation after generation as the several *husbands* before *Ailill* seem to attest. So, she (it/them) is in competition within her own herds and needs the breeding of external herds to maintain the potency of the cattle brothers and sisters. The idea of a bull spurning a woman because she is a woman (in the annals) is a very monkish sentiment.

As for *Cú Chullain* fighting one warrior after another and sustaining many wounds could this also be generational? It is important to note *Mórrigan* and her shapeshifting. Remember *she* is everything that the land is, from hares to falcons. *She* originally tempts him (we are never told how; we are left to assume the monks thought that, as a woman, she would offer him her body, poor celibate creatures that they were. He rejects *her* (the landscape of Connacht) so *she* transforms, again and again (eel, wolf, heifer), and is wounded each time.

What does this mean if we are to take the knowledge from the myth? Are we looking at times of hardship and food shortages? At the end of the story *she* presents herself as an *old woman*. Winter? Wisdom? *She* feeds him milk, three times (like the trefoil or thrice-blessing). Each time he accepts and with each acceptance *she* is healed of the wounds he previously inflicted.

Sometime later, as *Cú Chullain* licks his puppy wounds, a three (again) day battle occurs because the original *Fergus'* people have recovered from the sickness/curse. They fight a warrior called *Conchobar*, again not all it seems, because *Conchobar* is the offspring of *Ness* (the land itself, Ulaid or Ulster). *Ness* sired him with a druid because he (she/it/they) informed *her* that this particular day was a good one to conceive a *king* and he was the only *man* around. (Is it possible to uncover whether this is midwinter?) But she is the land and he is what? Con prefixing what? From what I could find the name *Conchobar* (and there have been many in Irish history) means dog or wolf lover. Remember we're not talking individual people here and *con* or *conn* means head, headland, intellect and/or chieftain.

At the end of this epic *Mabh* manages to get hold of the Brown Bull of Coolie (perhaps the animist symbol of Ulster) that fights and kills *Finnbhenn-ach*. The brown bull is mortally wounded, however, but apparently wanders Ireland naming places until his own death.

Would this entire story, when originally recited and passed from generation to generation, have meant something utterly different? Of course. It was not written until a thousand years of christian conquest. Can we learn its meaning? Does it matter in today's consumerist, attention-deprived wilderness of city, satellite and mobile phone?

As the mythic *Amairgin*[38] says in his epic song (from the *Lebor Gabála Érenn*): *I am the bull of seven battles.*

---

[38] Today, most scholars regard the *Lebor Gabála* as primarily myth rather than history.

While this breakdown is not at all meant to be a definitive reflection on the *Táin,* what it is hoped is that the reader so inclined delves into more than what is presented as childlike stories to explore the lore nesting within the legend. What are we really reading? What we should *not* be doing is interpreting it literally, like some fanatics do the christian bible, as that is playing right into the hands of those who would rather bequeath us a legacy of irrelevance.

Now we have a problem. With every story and every myth and every legend. We will never know our history from before the monks. New stories need to be born. When looking beyond the almost ridiculous tales represented in text, we are seeking commonalities to other words and, guessing really, at a depth we can no longer fully comprehend.

I go this deeply into the *Táin* as it and other stories are written of, ad nauseum, as being the legends of a people's past. That they be learned. Why? Many of the books I have read back up the status quo but... many of the recent sites I have visited make lots of profit as exponents of Celtic lore and as holders of workshops and chargers of much money for secret initiations into *true* bardic and druidic schools. It's now a business enterprise. Selling speculation and a feeling of belonging. Belonging to clan *is* to be nurtured and accepted but to be talked into accepting balderdash and to have to pay for it is outrageous.

PART 2

Big,

Big brown,

Big brown bear

Big brown bear blue bull...[39]

Why the learning of vast tracts of verse presented as song or story? Why was the *seanachaí*[40], the fíli, the ollamh,[41] the keeper of records and singers of verse, revered and anticipated?

Let me take you there: Just before Samhain, two thousand and fifty journeys around the sun ago, and you are amongst family and clan.

Since the end of summer all of you have gathered the food of the forest, hillside and heath. Hunted and slaughtered whatever cousins you could, furred, feathered or finned. Smoked as much as you could and stored it all deep beneath either the longhouse[42], a strong, dense wattle and daub structure in which your extended family and all your domesticated livestock will endure through the winter. Your hounds, your horses, your hunting eagles are also inside. Others on this hand-

---

[39] The Berenstains' B Book, Stan and Jane Berenstain
[40] (pronounced shahnahai) The word *seannachaí*, which was spelled *seanchaidhe* (plural *seanchaidhthe*) before the Irish-language' spelling reform of 1948, means a bearer of "old lore" (*seanchas*). In the ancient Celtic culture, the history and laws of the people were not written down but memorized in long lyric poems which were recited by bards (fíli), in a tradition echoed by the *seanchaithe*
[41] (pronounced *ollav*)
[42] Like the Neolithic long house built at Balbridie, Aberdeenshire, Scotland

raised hill fort, with its impassable ditches, live in smaller, but equally substantial dwellings that makes up your *túath*[43] or *finte*. What will not, however, close for the long nights are the forges and clan gatherings. Not unless the blizzards or the gales come.

Your beds are of thick straw, laced with autumn herbs and late-blooming flowers intended to dull the eventual stink of them. You and your extended family are about to be stuck with each other, the fat of cooking, the steam of boiling, body odor, the snores and farts and suckle of each other as well as the beasts; as you and they breed and bite and die, until the fires of *embibolgon*[44] when the drip, drop of melting snow, and the first bluebells, herald the big thaw. You have stacked wood to the rafters, dug peat by the ton, and ascertained all possibilities that the central fire pit will keep burning. Babies will be born here, women will die giving birth and the old man will also likely perish. At the long-toothed age of forty. You better have gathered sufficient supplies.

However...

You and your clans have been doing this for 75,000 years so you'll be fine. And there's enough fermented drink to see the worst ague mellowed. Stories will be taught and sung, as weapons are honed, furs piled, looms shuttled, and clay molded and fired. At the forges weapons and kettles will be hammered and shaped. At leisure, by the

---

[43] The social structure of ancient Irish culture was based around the concept of the *fine* (plural *finte*), or family kin-group. All *finte* descended from a common ancestor out to four generations comprised a social unit known as a *dearbhfhine* (plural *dearbhfhinte*). *Túatha* are often described as small kingdoms, whereas they are fortresses, as are duns (pronounced *doons*).

[44] Proto Celtic for "budding", later called Imbolg (pronounced *imelich*)

central hearth, hides will be chewed until supple, and sewn with fine bone needles, hung about with bear and beaver fur. The woman at the bench will twist ornate iron and gold-thread patterns, into torcs strong enough to save her son's and daughter's necks from a sword strike.

On Mona apprentices to the magical arts begin the training that will take them a lifetime to fully learn.

But before you enter the deep, dark of that long winter you travel. To what will one day be known as Avebury in Wiltshire, the territory of your wider clan, the Durotrig-ach. You, and much of the population, from the highlands and raven-hooded islands to the north, those of the *Eryr-ach* the perennially snowcapped mountains to the west, the Ecini and Cantiac-ach from the flat, marshy beaches and forests to the east and others, even further into the west, Dumnon-ach, miners of the tin. Us? Cutters of the chalk, diggers of the ditches, carvers and erectors of sarsen stone. Engineers.

And amongst the travelers are the lore-keepers of music, dreams, prophesy, dance, plant, heritage and stars. *Druí*. With them come the settlers of disputes, the Brehon judges, many of them, also chieftains. Someone sends for the elders to come, to cross the Menai from Inis Môn. Shadow men and shadow women, golden torcs, talismans of jet and amber, crane bags containing their medicine magic.

This is the celebration of harvest-home, the remembering and naming of mothers and fathers into the cold black peat of the past. Everyone dresses for the festival, adorned with finely-tanned, tooled and beaded leather, porcupine quill and gold, with elaborately sculpted coifs. Walrus bone pins hold hair, braided into crowns and piled atop the head, or else thick with lime, and shaped to mimic the plume of a high horse's tail.

Then the seanachaí come, the filí, the ollamh arrive.

They are here to recite the lineages of clan alliances and treaties agreed to, sometimes for centuries, sometimes for a thousand lifetimes, so that when *marriages* are agreed to all know what stock to expect. They sing of the ages, of the migrations of swan and swift, of the behavior of reindeer and boar, and they sing the children who will teach the hounds to hunt truffles and bring down the red deer.

They sing of that savage storm, four hundred years ago, that drowning an island outright, and upon it. They sing of who died, of their bravery and their mystery. Down there, within the chalk of the ditches where the acoustics carry their voices. That bard… what's her name? She sings the entire history of *immrama*, for forever it seems.

They recount, in song, lore that tell of the days the moon covered the sun and despair as entire herds succumbed to drought. The name of the lake that once touched the clouds, so they could bathe within her water—water that bubbled from deep beneath the surface of sight. Of massacres and finding strange lands with people of other-colored skin and what their boats looked like, how hot was the sun, how sweet was the fruit. And we all know the chorus, so we all sing it loudly.

But this year's-end the singer brings new stories, of people landing on our eastern shores and the murder they inflict. That no matter how hard we fought the strangers have not gone. Weeping, she sings their ways of torture. And we listen to new *eachtra,* adding them to the ancient knowledge. Remembering the chorus into them.

This is repeated by those gathered from across the land and by those who've traveled across the sea, and for hundreds of miles and who tell us of elephants and veiled women with kohl eyes and unreadable tattoos.

We exchange goods. Get drunk. We flirt and finally lay with each other, and when it's done, and everything is as it should be, we return to the long house for the dark. For the land of night where we can remind each other of what we have heard. To keep us from going crazy... and because it's so important to remember.

SPELLCRAFTING AND HOW THIS ALL WORKS

Ringa ringa rosies,
A pocket full of posies,
A'tissue, a'tissue,
We all fall down. (The black plague)

Thirty days hath September, April, June and November...
(remembering how long each month is on the Gregorian calendar)

Humpty Dumpty sat on the wall, Humpty Dumpty had a great fall... (it was a canon, not an egg)
In Reading Gaol by Reading town
There is a pit of shame,
And in it lies a wretched man
Eaten by teeth of flame,
In burning winding-sheet he lies,
And his grave has got no name. (True story. More to the point it was about

Wilde being imprisoned for homosexuality)

To

All in all it's just another brick in the wall.
All in all you're just another brick in the wall.[45] (protest)

And, no less, David Bowie, *Space Oddity*, 1969, who sang:
This is Major Tom to Ground Control
I'm stepping through the door
And I'm floating in a most peculiar way
And the stars look very different today
For here
Am I sitting in a tin can
Far above the world
Planet Earth is blue
And there's nothing I can do.

Because that same year (1969) the first astronauts launched into space, and the Apollo Two landing module, the *Eagle*, dropped a couple of men onto the surface of the moon, people could be mistaken into thinking the song was related to that event in some way, but there is a deeper meaning, and they were wrong. Bowie saw the movie *2001, A Space Odyssey* several times that year, stoned, as he says, each time. And under the influence of (at least) that drug, the story had a

---

[45] Pink Floyd, The Wall

profound and inspirational affect. Bowie was *Major Tom*. Ten years later, after a cocaine addiction that almost killed him, he released *Ashes to Ashes*, however, and liberates himself from *Major Tom*, getting clean. He was, as a result, awarded custody of his son:

Ashes to ashes

Funk to funky

We know Major Tom's a junkie

Strung out in heaven's high

Hitting an all-time low.

Every true bard, poet, songwriter inspires not *only* because of the majesty of the story but because they expose deep, profound aspects of themselves, life, observation that give us permission to also do so. They give us courage. They share our despair. They remind us of something. They are mirrors to our own life struggles. Who is to say this has not always been so? Do we not feel it in our bones? We care. We are touched. It *has* always been so. As the ancient bards told epic tales of heroes so, also, did Freddy Mercury sing *We are the Champions.*

And let's not kid ourselves, the poet, the songwriter, the satirist is to be feared. They are the artists and witches who can bring down kings, popes, pedophiles and politicians. They are the only people we go to for the truth in anything likely to be a lie; anything that sincerely requires our attention. As when Billie Holliday sang:

Southern trees bear strange fruit

Blood on the leaves and blood at the root

Black bodies swinging in the southern breeze

Strange fruit hanging from the poplar trees[46]

Every culture learns this way. If ever we stop, we will forget everything.

PART 3

"I am the cave in which my mother's body lies
I am the soldier who cries, and packs of hunting dogs
I am the dance within the secret games of children
And the storm wreck on the shoreline of a bay
I'm the hammer and the clay
I am the wild host and the midden
I am here and I am somewhere other than.
I am never known to linger and yet I stay
Who am I?
Who am I not?[47]"

---

[46] *Strange Fruit*, written by Abel Meeropol, most famously sung by both Billie Holiday and Nina Simone

[47] Ly de Angeles, *Initiation | a Memoir*, 2016

Animism encompasses the understanding that all material phenomena have agency, that there exists no hard and fast distinction between the spiritual and physical (or material) world and that soul or spirit or sentience exists not only in humans, but also in other animals, plants, rocks, geographic features such as mountains, and rivers or other entities of the natural environment including thunder, wind, snow,
wildfire and shadows. Animism thus rejects Cartesian dualism. Animism may further attribute soul to abstract concepts such as words, true names or metaphors in mythology.

ANIMISM – *LORE*

The *Challenge of Amergin* (below), spoken or sung when the legendary bard of the Milesians *clann Mhíle*, (invented by monks or not), landed on the shores of Éire approximately 1286BCE (from the early 17th century *Annals of the Four Masters*) is then not so mysterious after all.

Many accounts of what is recited are called arrogant because of an utter lack, on behalf of christianized monks, chroniclers, scholars and academics, into the current era, to recognize animism. Amergin is meeting and merging with what the Australian First Nation people call *Country*. The bards and all with them provide the landscape with their breath and the recitation of all that is. A two-way conversation, both honoring the experience of being and through the words, remembering mnemonically for future generations.

"*I am the wind on the sea,*
I am the wave of the sea,
I am the bull of seven battles,

I am the eagle on the rock
I am a flash from the sun;
I am the most beautiful of plants,
I am a strong wild boar,
I am a salmon in the water,
I am a lake in the plain,
I am the word of knowledge,
I am the head of the spear in battle,
I am the god that puts fire in the head,
Who spreads light in the gathering on the hills?
Who can tell the ages of the moon?
Who can tell the place where the sun rests?

The above is only one of many interpretations from *The Book of Invasions* or *Leabhar Gabhála na hÉireann*, a compendium of history, folklore, and mythology in prose and poetry form. Work compiled by an anonymous scholar around the 11th century and purporting to be a true history of Ireland whereas, in fact, it is a pseudo-history with christian and pre-christian mythological elements, telling of wave after wave of invasion and immigration into Ireland. It is preserved in several manuscripts, including the *Book of Leinster* and the *Book of Lecan*, copies of which can be found at the Royal Irish Academy and Trinity College Dublin. Declaring words akin to *terra nullius*[48].and that no one lived in Ireland before outsiders rocked up, despite vast evidence to the contrary.

---

[48] Latin: *nobody's land*

Note in the above, when discussing Amergin, I am gender-neutral. The sexism inherent in translation is repugnant. Indigenous cultures do not use the words man/woman, male/female, masculine/feminine. We only have relationships: mother, father, aunt, sister, brother, friend, cousin.

In his diaries, Tacitus wrote of the lack of gender-bias, just prior to the crushing defeat of Boudica and the tribal confederacies that fought with her: *[The Britons] make no distinction of gender in their leaders.*

In *War and Gender,* Joshua Goldstein writes: "Boudica took leadership of the Iceni people (in present-day England) after her husband died. Her Iron Age society was of Celtic heritage (see p. 115) – warlike, reckless, horse-loving, robust and strong, prone to fighting naked accompanied by loud noise and frequent drinking. Celtic women, although they did not rule in a matriarchy, led freer lives than Roman law allowed. Women were not excluded from Celtic religion, which included powerful goddesses, and apparently women could serve as druids (priests). The historian Tacitus said of the Britons (in contrast to the Romans), "they make no distinction of sex in their appointment of commanders.""

Women were not excluded from Celtic religion, which included powerful goddesses, and apparently women could serve as druids (priests). Biased and thoughtless.

All written material pertaining to the Britons come to us through the lens of Roman chroniclers and later through successive patriarchal scholarship. Why does he not write that women were included, and by the term *goddess* does he infer genius loci? Or are we, again, stuck with anthropomorphism?

Tacitus, *Annals, Book Fourteen, Chapter 30.* [The Druids at Mona Island]: "On the opposite shore stood the Britons, close embodied, and prepared for action. Women were seen running through the ranks in wild disorder; their apparel funeral[49]; their hair loose to the wind, in their hands flaming torches, and their whole appearance resembling the frantic rage of the Furies. The Druids were ranged in order, with hands uplifted, invoking the gods, and pouring forth horrible imprecations. The novelty of the fight struck the Romans with awe and terror. They stood in stupid amazement, as if their limbs were benumbed, riveted to one spot, a mark for the enemy. The exhortations of the general diffused new vigor through the ranks, and the men, by mutual reproaches, inflamed each other to deeds of valor. They felt the disgrace of yielding to a troop of women, and a band of fanatic priests; they advanced their standards and rushed on to the attack with impetuous fury."

---

[49] In Britain white was the color of mourning until the 19th Century. Black would have had other connotations such as night and shadow and soot used in tattooing. The use of "funeral" is in the translation into English. Some monk's idea of propriety.

Centuries later we are given the Welsh story of how Gwion Bach accidentally gained the three drops of wisdom meant for Ceridwen's *ugly* son. After, both shapeshift through many forms, and the seeds of wisdom are transformed into the birth of someone/thing else (in the stories a newborn human infant) and sent down river. This could be time or generations. It could also represent years of training in bardic work. The result is that the child is found and is so beautiful it is called *Taliesin* (meaning *shining brow*). Anyone can find the history of this person, always alluded to as "he" and you will read, in many sources,
that he became Merlin, magician to the purely fictional Arthur[50]. *Taliesin's* poems. however, were written in the 6th century, in a by now utterly christianized Wales.

    I propose that all non-Abrahamic afterlife stories are actually all seasonal, but I leave that exploration to others. What *does* interest me is why, in the 21st century of Celto/European consciousness and education, these stories remain important? What use are they unless they are deconstructed to inform proper and respectful ways of living and thriving as earth?

---

[50] *Arthur* is Latin for bear. It is not a British/Welsh name. Worth the hunt. No such person

The problem we face is that schools and individuals repeat the same information. All gender their deities, write of *gods* and *goddesses,* and they are named, just like Aunty Violet or Maude Gonne or Elizabeth Taylor, so the reader or student gets the sense that they are single-minded individuals. Or were, because even though reconstructed in the current times, and popular amongst people referring to themselves as pagans, druids, Celts, Vikings, witches, revivalists—stories and texts are all written of in the past tense. Are we, then, to assume that deities cease once people stop believing in them? Perhaps, though, as I suggested in the Preamble, Neil Gaimon's *American Gods*, become all-too plausible.

The Celts are written to have an *otherworld.* Also, an *underworld.* Written, in the current era, to be accessed by the living at the time of the ancient festival of Samhain, when the *veils are thinnest between the worlds of life and death, and the ancestors are invited to the feast.* But there's nothing scholarly, and nothing written that isn't recently invented,
supposedly based on older stories. There is no ancestral continuity. The non-literate, oral custom of storytelling was obfuscated, alongside our culture and languages, only to be documented by monks who would have been versed, at best, only in Latin or Greek, therefore trapping the stories on vellum, scribed with ancient ink, and by whatever slant the penman was skewed.

Where is *between the worlds*? Is it the dreaming? Could be. The *Underworld*? Is it the initiate's experience with psychoactive *immram* in the caves and barrows of their elders? Could easily be. Because we are still doing these things. We are not a new people. We can never fully know the truth about deep time, but we can come close. But only by understanding the *way* of learning utilized by indigenous people, pretty-much worldwide, without misappropriation.

But let us continue with referencing the Celto/Gaelic influence.

REWILDING LANGUAGE

(because language defines a culture)

We live in an age of forgetting. Suffering what George Monbiot, in his book *Feral*, describes as *shifting baseline syndrome* in relation to an ecological habitat. The syndrome is denial that anything has ever been other than the way we understand it from a recent historic perspective.

To even begin to contemplate *who* we are, and to therefore gather around us cousins of all species, we must conjure an indigenous language and an individual voice to both storytelling and self. To do so is to remove such words as: god/goddess (that are gendered and not relative to the preamble, deity, demon, sacrifice, AD (for the year), altar, amen, OMG, belief, salvation, celebrant, celibacy, sabbatical, retreat, chakra, karma, channeling, christmas, easter, hallow'een, even the word religion except in context, angel, unless in its Greek etymology of *messenger*, tiny, harmless, winged fairies.

I include in this context military jargon—war—in this clean-up of our language. "They conquered Everest." "They fought boldly but the cancer won the battle and they died." "Those brave men who sacrificed their lives for their country." Because, no they didn't. Those people called soldiers died brutally, killed strangers with no unbiased realization of why. Very often they were and are maimed for life and commit atrocities onto people of every species and place, including the dropping of atomic bombs on two major Japanese cities, the "shock and awe" propaganda and destruction that has pretty-much continued since the first attack on Iraq under that title, and the deforestation of entire landscapes. Therefore, please stop using the word *lumber* for trees and *human resources* (that's a newey) for people.

Soul is okay[51] but requires discourse.

LANGUAGE AND CULTURE

So, to *bandraíodóir*[52].

Caillea-ch[53] (as a word because it is not a name) is interesting, but not in the way most every site online, and most books describes it. *Calleach* is purported to be an anthropomorphic female deity. As an old hag. There is a wild promontory on the cliffs of Moher, Ireland, named Ceann Caillí interpreted as Hag's Head, also, in Scotland *Cailleach Bheur(ach)* and is associated with winter. Argyle's *Cruachan* (Cruachan Mountain) is said to be the home of *Cailleach nan Cruachan*. Thinking as an animist, however, we can remove the androcentric association and realize that Ben[54] Cruachan *is Cailleach nan Cruachan*. Can you see what I see that? All the places named for Cailleach are *high*.

When ascertaining the potential threat of invasion or attack where do people want to be? High. Where they can see in a 360° circle. Also, in the cycle of a year winter always comes. There's been *so* much lost in translation.

The many ridiculous tales, from that patrician old man in the sky, from his poor tortured son and that son's virginal mother ascending,

---

[51] Sometimes said to mean originally 'coming from or belonging to the sea,' because that was supposed to be the stopping place of the soul before birth or after death [Barnhart]; if so, it would be from Proto-Germanic *saiwaz*. Klein explains this as "from the lake," as a dwelling-place of souls in ancient northern Europe.
[52] Enchantress, woman druid, shapeshifter
[53] As the circle, mistranslated as old hag, or ugly old woman
[54] A *ben* is mountain: *beanna*

literally on a cloud, to that poor tortured son's lover living out the remainder of her life in a cave in Baum, France, drinking only her own tears for sixty years until she, too, ascends. There is no animism and as such real stories of weather gods, seasonal gods, gods of place have been belittled and dishonored. And the animists, the people of this knowledge, humiliated and called barbarians, and history writ by those believing themselves far superior when that's transparent ignorance.

In the *hag* testaments the *old woman* bit comes in because *hag* has an etymology: Early 13C: *repulsive old woman* (rare before 16C.) probably from Old English hægtes, hægtesse *witch, sorceress, enchantress, fury*. Dutch *heks,* German *Hexe witch*. The disambiguation is due, mistakenly, to a later Anglo-Saxon interpretation that, by then woman-shaming christianised monastics could not get their tonsures around. That of an animist language. To me the idea of winter as a person, with moods and mists and personality, is obvious.

English is a language of objectification. The language assumes there's us, and that everything else is *out there*. A language of nouns.

Dr. Robin Wall Kimmerer is a mother, scientist, writer, and Distinguished Teaching Professor of Environmental Biology at the SUNY College of Environmental Science and Forestry in Syracuse, New York. She is the founding Director of the Center for Native Peoples and the Environment; whose mission is to create programs that draw on the wisdom of both indigenous and scientific knowledge for our shared concerns for Mother Earth. She works at learning her language alongside her sister. She found it extremely difficult until she *grokked* it. She writes, in the essay *The Grammar of Animacy*: "To be a hill, to be a sandy beach, to be a Saturday, all are possible verbs in a world where everything is alive. Water, land, and even a day, the language a mirror for seeing the animacy of the world, the life that pulses through all things, through pines and nuthatches and mushrooms. THIS is the language I hear in the woods, this is the language that lets us speak of what wells up all around us. And the vestiges of boarding schools, soap-wielding missionary wraiths, hang their heads in defeat.⁵⁵"

Thus, realizing this, we return to Celtic/Gaelic and we learn that our word *calleach* is two words:

    The first part of the word *call, caill* or *cor*, means circle, as in *coracle*, a round boat. The end of the word, *ach* (pronounced as soft, like loch), is abstract but profound: the etymology (from Old Irish *-ach*, from Proto-Celtic *ākos*, compare Welsh -og. Doublet of -óg. Suffix **–ach:** *Forms nouns from other nouns and adjectives with the sense of 'person or thing connected or involved with, belonging to, having, as'*, "Person or thing⁵⁶ connected or involved with, belonging to, having, as."

Éire (Ireland) + -ach⟶ Éireannach (*as* Ireland), Sasana (England)+ -ach⟶ Sasanach (*as* England), Albanachⁱ, for example is a person (no matter the species) from Alba. We are the landscape. An ancient way of knowing still extant within indigenous people's language: "*To be a hill, to be a sandy beach, to be a Saturday, all are possible verbs in a world where everything is alive.:*

---

⁵⁵ http://www.dailygood.org/more.php?n=6819
⁵⁶ A *thing* is an ancient word for a gathering; an assembly of people for multiple purposes. It does not mean an object with no name
https://www.historyonthenet.com/viking-law-and-government-the-thing/

If you feel to go back to the *Táin Bó Cúalnge* and reexamine names, with this in mind, you will find a deeper, more inclusive story.

This is a way of knowing and *being* in relationship with place and season, weather and time. It is us as landscape and history. What the Yanyuwa, the human people of the Gulf Carpentaria in Northern Australia, call *kujika*: "...it is so beautifully clear that these songs give an intensive knowledge of the geography for navigation and identification and behavioural details of the animals in each microenvironment.[57]"

. . .

---

[57] http://www.lynnekelly.com.au/2014/11/singing-the-knowledge-yanyuwa-kujika/

CASE: THE ISLE OF LEWIS (OUTER HEBRIDES)

The Callanish Stones are the standing stones on the Isle of Lewis. Lewis is the Anglicization of *Leòdhas*[58], which in modern Scots Gaelic has been said to derive from *leogach*, which means marshy, BUT if we take the suffix *leogh,* and presume it means marshy, then the people of the island are the *ach* compound of the word. Consequently, Callanish is two words: Call (as in Calledon-ach) and not *ish* but *ach* we are using the local and ancient parlance that simply says, 'stone circle'. I also mention the work of Gordon C Harrison's site, *Landscapes For You*[59], when, discussing Lewis, he writes: "Can also be written as Lews. In Gaelic it is Leòdhas or Leòdh' and it appears in the Norse sagas[60] as Ljóðhús. There is some doubt about the true origin of this name but most toponymists have decided it is of Norse origin, derived from Ljóða-hús meaning 'house of songs or lays' in other words a céildh house."

That island, along with many of the Outer Hebrides, was invaded/colonized by the Norse (commonly called Vikings[61]) around 900 CE. They never left. The Albanach reclaimed it but the merger of the two peoples was long established. By love or rape or agreement, who knows? The ditch around the circle of stones is as large as that of

---

[58] *Leòdhas:* the dh is silent
[59] http://www.gordon-c-harrison.co.uk/About-Folder/Scottish-Place-Names/Place-Names-F-L
[60] A "saga" (Norse/Icelandic) means something said, a narrative.
[61] Scandinavian pirate, 1801, *vikingr*, http://www.etymonline.com/word/viking

both Stonehenge and Avebury, attesting to the probability of it also being used as an oratory space.

Human have been proven to have lived on the island for at least 8,000 years but, according to archaeologists the stones were not put in place before 2,900CE. "The first traces of human activity are indicated by a broad ditch (no longer visible above ground) which appears to have belonged to some structure or enclosure.[62]"

THIS is profoundly important when we take Dr. Lynne Kelly's research of mnemonics into account. And yet it is a throwaway line on a Wiki site.

Of Stonehenge's vast ditch (also that of Durrington Walls) being used for oration of song and story, learning and poetry, with great acoustics, Dr. Kelly writes: "It struck me that if the elders were performing at the base of the ditch, not amongst the menhirs, then the shape of the ditch would work as a theatre.[63]"

Today's druids are genealogists. Their work is guiding us home. Away from the shadowland of *shifting baseline syndrome* and above the snowline into the forests of fur and fungi, spruce and oak silence, or else the ack-ack of ravens, that are our inheritance and our kin. Our dignity.

---

[62] https://en.wikipedia.org/wiki/Callanish_Stones#Archaeology_and_dating
[63] The Memory Code (p. 110)

My own family has been traced to almost 2000 years before now; we are our Irish ancestors whose wellspring is Connacht, the lands of *Mabh*. We have a mother in 12th century Paris, musicians, poets and ardrí of *Dál Riata*, Albanach, and the bones of a thousand lifetimes of women who are Brittany. Since coming to know my ancestry I have

spoken with many Anglo-Europeans about their own. Except for indigenous knowledge-holders, the furthest back anyone I have asked remembers, occasionally, are the names of great grandparents. That is changing with the internet. With accessible sources to records. Once-sealed doors into crypts of parchments and drunk priest's margin notes are currently open We must descend quickly before something untoward slams them shut again.

To my great astonishment many do not understand the significance of this recollection or even consider it relevant.

It is.

We are earth. We are made of stars and we have forgotten our relationship with both the universe and kindred species. This is madness on a grand scale. It allows for the wholesale destruction of the habitats of others, the cruelty of factory farming, the negligence of overusing antibiotics and force-feeding of hormones, the sheer mountains and islands of toxic waste to the terrible detriment of world-wide future health, to the hurricanes and wildfires currently unleashing havoc and terror. In readiness for a reckoning.

I have no doubt Dr Karen Adams[64], in an ABC discussion[65] for NAIDOC[66] Week, July 2016 was utterly well-meaning when she said:

"My very early memories of being on country are the names of towns in Gippsland. For instance, Tooradin, and its name basically means a swamp monster. And Koo Wee Rup, another little tiny town in Gippsland means place of plenty of blackfish or baskets of blackfish…. knowing what those names mean creates a much deeper connection to place… this is a swamp and there's mangroves and the swamp's stagnant mud that has a very distinct smell. And I think knowing that history and knowing that there have been artefacts found in Tooradin that are 30,000 years old, that there is a very old, old history in that country and a story in that country. And I think that all Australians should take a great deal of pride in that, because of Aboriginal culture we have these continuing stories to our country that other countries actually don't have. I think that that's something to be really proud about."

But this knowledge is not *our* knowledge. This knowledge is that of the Gunaikurnai Nation, a confederacy of five major clans. However, the region called Gippsland is named after an officer in Queen Victoria's armed forces named George Gipps. It is not named for the Gunaikurnai Nation. Also, concerning this, is Angus McMillan[67]:

"1840 - Nuntin- unknown number killed by Angus McMillan's men

---

[64] Associate Professor, Medical and Health Science, Monash University, Melbourne and http://www.monash.edu/medicine/about-us/indigenous-health
[65] http://www.abc.net.au/radionational/programs/allinthemind/indigenous-memory-code/7553976#transcript
[66] National Aborigines and Islanders Day Observance Committee

[67] https://en.wikipedia.org/wiki/Angus_McMillan

1840 - Boney Point – "Angus McMillan and his men took a heavy toll of Aboriginal lives"

1841 - Butchers Creek - 30-35 shot by Angus McMillan's men

1841 - Maffra - unknown number shot by Angus McMillan's men

1842 - Skull Creek - unknown number killed

1842 - Bruthen Creek – "hundreds killed"

1843 - Warrigal Creek - between 60 and 180 shot by Angus McMillan and his men

1844 - Maffra - unknown number killed

1846 - South Gippsland - 14 killed

1846 - Snowy River - 8 killed by Captain Dana and the Aboriginal Police

1846-47 - Central Gippsland - 50 or more shot by armed party hunting for a white woman supposedly held by Aborigines; no such woman was ever found

1850 - East Gippsland - 15-20 killed

1850 - Murrindal - 16 poisoned

1850 - Brodribb River - 15-20 killed"

Angus McMillan was born in 1810 on the Isle of Skye, Scotland. What was happening then were the 19th century Clearances. The inhabitants of Skye, from whence McMillan's family hailed, were also devastated by famine. Thirty thousand people were evicted between 1840 and 1880 alone with many of them forced to emigrate.

I suggest he was a bitter, haughty, savage man doing whatever he could to establish himself as a laird in this new colonial outpost because he was driven from his own ancestral home, named for a family that were, once upon a time, Scottish royalty. How low had his family fallen that they must take to a transport ship and invade another people's ancestral land? Murder them? What kind of iniquity then, when in 1949, an entire region of the state of Victoria is named for him: The District of McMillan? How cruel an injustice perpetrated onto the First Nation people, whose ancestors and whose songlines are
that landscape and every rock and lizard and mangrove and blackfish?

In 1846 Gippsland squatter Henry Meyrick wrote in a letter home to his relatives in England: *The blacks are very quiet here now, poor wretches. No wild beast of the forest was ever hunted down with such unsparing perseverance as they are. Men, women and children are shot whenever they can be met with… I have protested against it at every station I have been in Gippsland, in the strongest language, but these things are kept very secret as the penalty would certainly be hanging … For myself, if I caught a black actually killing my sheep, I would shoot him with as little remorse as I would a wild dog, but no consideration on earth would induce me to ride into a camp and fire on them indiscriminately, as is the custom whenever the smoke is seen. They [the Aborigines] will very shortly be extinct. It is impossible to say how many have been shot, but I am convinced that not less than five hundred have been murdered altogether.*[68]"

---

[68] https://en.wikipedia.org/wiki/Gunai

A story to be retold. So that it slaps deniers in the face and allows the Anglo-Saxon/Europeans to grow up. When Dr. Adams says, "And I think that all Australians should take a great deal of pride in that, because of Aboriginal culture we have these continuing stories to our country that other countries actually don't have. I think that that's something to be really proud about." I shudder. I feel my body being covered with white-tailed spiders. Because of *shifting baseline syndrome*.

INDOCTRINATION & EDUCATION vs. LEARNING

History must be remembered. In context. I don't want to learn about ancient Greece or ancient Rome. How marvelous they were. I don't need to learn of the wheat and sheep and coal that I was burdened with in high school and that my daughter was burdened to have to learn about a generation later. I don't want to hear the praises and genealogies of the English monarchy or the dates of the Battle of This or the Battle of That because they are not our battles. We are not taught of our own struggles, as indigenous Irish or indigenous Albanach, indigenous Britons, to hold ancient clan lands from those very people we are taught deserve our respect. And because we are *indoctrinated* with all the conflicting stories of the conquerors of our sovereign ancestral territories. We are not taught *why* they burned our forests to the ground on Mona, because we are not taught about the Scottish Clearances or the *why* of the Dublin Massacres of 1916, we know nothing of ourselves.

We were not told that we could possibly be our ancient lands. We were made to stand in lines, in uniform, and sing God Save the Queen. We never knew that bears and wolves, lynx, elephants, the golden eagle, otters, eels and badgers might be the totems of our clans; that they roamed us as mountains and swam in us as lakes in abundance. We were kept from the truth of the fireballs flung at our kindred by ballista, and that entire environments and populations were decimated. Even in high school I was not informed that Gráinne Mhaol, more commonly known as Gráinuaile, the so-called pirate queen (in reality, a chieftain), had met Elizabeth Tudor with knives in her boots, or taught that Pádraig Piarais, a school teacher, philosopher and poet had lead the aforementioned doomed *Easter Uprising*, in Dublin, to end the scourge of British occupation.

I never learned of Bobby Sands, who died of starvation along with several other men, in an action known as *troscadh*[69], a pre-christian tradition whereby a wronged person would fast outside the home of the transgressor, relying on strong indigenous traditions of hospitality to force justice. We never got the truth of *why* Protestants and Catholics fought. We were never taught that the British displaced the Irish by colonizing the north of the country with disenfranchised Scots. We thought the expression of outrage, *Beyond the Pale*, just meant a thing was not good enough.

---

[69] Hunger strike

We wrote in our little books, like puppets, the history that Captain Cook *discovered* this land that would eventually be called Australia, a name that is no name at all, simply meanings *southern land/* That the imperialism that later forged states and territories only ever named them for an invading monarchy. And, as any of us who have journeyed southern Wales can attest New South Wales bears no resemblance other than that sections of the landscape are mountainous. Obscured utterly was the fact that this vast island was once peopled with untold Aboriginal tribes, many of whom traded with the Makassan of Indonesia for countless hundreds of years, long before Cook turned up, and who, in arrogant gall. claimed another's land as belonging to a distant queen and planting the Butcher's Apron in the sand of the cove lived on by the Gweagal people of the Dharawal Nation. The British continue to claim, gouge, displace and sell off vast quantities of this island that is not, and never will be, theirs.

I was not to know of Truganini, a royal woman of the decimated Oyster Cove tribe in Tasmania. That her mother was killed by sailors, her uncle shot by a soldier, her sister abducted by sealers, and her love slaughtered by loggers, who then repeatedly sexually abused her. Truganini who lived from approximately 1812 to 1876, only to have her skeleton dragged from its grave and displayed in a museum.

ANGER

Anger does not have to be violent, but it must be heard, because it is never reasonless. Anger always has a source. I am first generation born in this landscape not of my bones, and I was to live many decades not knowing this, having been adopted at birth by strangers. My PARC mediator eventually provided me with birth certificates of a female biological parent, and the birth certificates and marriage certificates of both of her parents. I learned of a family that exists in every cell of my bones. I had already lived much of my adult life roaming and hunting ghost-forests of long-lived Celtic lands of Britain. Of Ireland. Of spectral duns in the highlands of Alba and the coastlines of modern-day Brittany. Stolen from the tribes of the Briganti, the Catuvellauni, the Audui, Carnute, Meldi, Secusian, Boli, Senones, Aulerc and many others. Their fate? Either bend the knee to Rome or perish.

I hadn't known because for fifty-five years I'd been lied to.

How can the subjugation and slaughter, the humiliation and indignity, sometimes the outright genocide, by the British or any other self-proclaimed *empire*, of untold native people, ever be justified?

So, I am angry. Anger that is wholly and full-frontally justified. Does it destroy? No. It seeks. It researches every oozing wound that will never heal until the truth is both realized and acknowledged. For that to happen all of us must know who we are. That the Gunaikurnai Nation, or any of the indigenous people of this country, survived and regained themselves should have been impossible. Because of so much ruthlessness. That the region known as Gippsland is not immediately renamed is to the shame of every person who has come here without permission. Since an English sailor brought the first shipments of slaves (called convicts), sent to this often-hostile, never-home landscape, from the slums and poverty imposed on its 'own' people, to get on with the business of the Anglo-Saxon crown (a royalty that has no indigenous name), much injustice and ignorance remains continuous.

Time to remember. Time to question everything we have been force-fed.

2

MIDWINTER SOLSTICE

LORE

THE POWER'S BEEN ON AND OFF all day. It's a good thing the boss decided the open fire would please the customers. Pub's been packed all night, everybody trying to keep warm.

'Lot of people gonna freeze in this weather,' says Fergus as he locks the doors on the last of the patrons before the patrol cars cruise their rounds and fine him for being open after hours.

'Go on home, Rowan.' He comes back and starts shifting the last of the glasses into the dishwasher, 'and be careful out there – the cold's bloody tragic.'

No one has ever known the temperature to get this low and

everybody in the pub had talked about little else.

'Weird,' someone said.

'Unnatural, I reckon,' said another. 'Scientists have gone and played around with it,' had been the reply.

Yep. People going to die on a night like this. I throw on my extra sweater and load myself with coat and beanie and gloves and scarf.

'G'night boss,' I call over my shoulder, pulling open the door onto the street, slamming it locked behind me.

It's like walking into a furnace only the other way around. The wind tears at my coat, sleet bites into my eyes. I have to stop and pull my scarf up over my mouth and nose so that I can even breathe. I start the seven-block walk to home, cursing wherever the cabs have all gone.

I work hard just to put one foot in front of the other. I can't feel my feet and I'm only managing to keep my hands even slightly warm by shoving them into my armpits. Even the scarf around my face feels frozen after a minute.

Move somewhere else, I say to myself, but then I've been saying that for years and have never been able to come up with enough money or enough courage to do it. No work anywhere else anyway – not in this city, not in any, anymore.

Three AM's a bitch, I think.

I ignore the DON'T WALK signs at the street crossings and I have a laugh cause no one else is stupid enough to be out on a night like this. Street's deader than the grave, even with christmas just four days away.

I've just crossed over Market Street and I'm about to turn into Left

Bank Road, that leads onto the turnoff to the last five blocks to my place (two rooms above the Chinese Cafe down by the canal) when this big guy moves out of the alley and blocks my way.

I'm freaked. I look up into coal-black eyes, pinning me to the spot.

He's easy six-two, six-three, bundled in a big old army greatcoat. I can't figure out if he has layers and layers of clothes underneath or whether he's just plain huge. Dark skin, little plaited beard, no hat, ragged dreadlocks hanging halfway to his waist studded all through with black feathers.

I don't know if he's going to kill me, rob me or try to bum a cigarette, but whatever blood's left unfrozen in my veins kinda just freezes altogether and I don't know whether I could run even if my legs weren't shaking, or whether my bladder's just going to end up embarrassing me.

'Wh–?' I stammer, 'Ah, 'scuse me.'

My attempt at being casual – at walking around him – is blocked as he moves his bulk and puts a hand on my arm to prevent any attempt to avoid him.

'Name's Hunter,' he says softly, deeply. 'Need your help. Got a job for you.' His eyes are like the eyes of a raptor.

I'm not about to get out of this, I think flatly. The wind's ripping and jagging all around him but the big man's body is blocking it from tearing at me.

'What?' I say, resigned. He takes hold of the sleeve of my coat and walks me into the alley. I never go this way; have no idea where it leads. There's garbage and refuse, pallets and dead cars, dumpsters and stacks of boxes – refugees from the back of unknown shops.

We're walking for several minutes. *This place is a bloody maze,* I think. It's a warren of twisting turns, back alleys leading into other back alleys, no idea where I am. Hoping this guy knows where he's going 'cause I sure don't. Wondering whether he's just dragging out the inevitability of some weirdo perversity.

Five, ten minutes, it takes us. Black as pitch.

Hunter seems sure of where he's going. Walls like prisons all around. Frozen to the marrow by now.

He jerks me to a stop and slides open a big heavy door. He flicks a switch and the boxy little entrance is lit up dimly by a naked bulb hanging from a wire suspended from the low ceiling. He wrenches the rusty industrial door closed and flips the bar locked.

'What's your name, son?' he asks, as he reaches under his coat and pulls out a small red plastic flashlight.

'Ah, it's Rowan. I'm Rowan. Wh-what's going on?' I feel like rabbit stuck in the lights of an oncoming truck. And I still can't feel my feet.

'Thought it'd be you,' says Hunter. He hasn't smiled yet.

'How serious is this?' I ask.

'You know,' he replies.

I'm really frustrated; starting not to feel so afraid any more.

'What are you talking about,' I yell. Is this guy some crazy?

'Don't raise your voice.' He grabs my face in his enormous hand and squeezes my cheeks. 'Just–'

Oh, oh, I think.

'Look,' he sighs, 'just don't raise your voice okay?' And he lets go.

'Sorry,' he says softly, 'let's just keep going okay?'

We start down the stairs. Soon the light from the top landing gets lost in the darkness and Hunter flicks on the torch. There's a sense of urgency comes at me from him. He's hurrying.

In the constantly moving swathe of the torch's light the place looks like the kind of place that used to lead to trains or something. Same smell but unused – mold or damp or something else living in the dark. Old tiles on the walls in places, or else that disgusting grey-green paint that nobody uses anymore. The stairs are just concrete. I feel like I'm going to die here. A man-made tomb a long way down.

Hunter's not talking, and I'd rather not think – it's too late and I'm too unnerved. I start counting steps between the landings – twenty-nine, landing's thirty; twenty-nine, landing's thirty. Fifth lot down and we're at the bottom.

The beam from the flashlight makes the dark feel like some kind of monster.

'Shit, I'd never make a miner,' I say, just to break the unbelievably dense silence. A hint of laughter rumbles from deep in his chest..

Alright. I think. *Breakthrough.*

We're on the platform of some abandoned part of the Underground. We drop down onto the tracks and Hunter leads us into one of the tunnels.

'Watch your step,' he says, shining the beam onto the ground. The tracks are littered with chunks of rubble. He throws the light up onto the wall and I can see how the whole lot looks like it could cave in any minute and great slabs have already fallen off. Yeah, I'll be quiet.

We walk maybe a hundred yards down the tunnel before I notice the warm, yellow light just up ahead to the left.

We get to the entrance of what looks like a service bay and Hunter jumps up onto the ledge, pulling me up behind him. It's a cavernous concrete room lit by dozens of candles and a few kerosene storm lanterns.

My mouth drops open as I look around, aware of a momentary whimper from somewhere.

First few seconds:

The original fixtures of the service bay are still here – a thick cloth hose with a dull brass nozzle, wound up and hanging from one wall beside several hooks; bench underneath it. Shelves line the back wall with old paint tins, jars and rusted stuff that I don't recognize; an antique metal and laminated table in the corner with cups and plates, a half-empty jar of instant coffee, sugar and a carton of milk, a three-ring cooker attached to a gas bottle on the floor beneath the table, other things. A tap and a sink against the other wall and what looks like an old kerosene fridge.

Someone's scrounged up furniture. There's an overstuffed three-seater settee covered in dark brown velvet, pretty thread-bare mostly, in the middle of the room, right beside a cut down forty-four-gallon drum with holes knocked into it, glowing red and sending out a welcome haze of warmth. Beside it is a tub over-flowing with bits of wood and scavenged timber.

In front of the settee someone's organized a couple of crates and planks that make up a squat table, and there's an assortment of straight-backed chairs and a couple of arm-chairs on this side of the table.

Over by the other wall are several mattresses, their bedding and pillows in disarray attesting to the fact that there's probably more than just Hunter staying down here. He's stripping off his coat and gloves and piling them just inside the entrance. I follow his lead.

'Okay,' I start, 'Can you please tell me—'

He ignores me as a small moan, followed by rapid breathing, breaks the silence of the room and Hunter strides quickly over towards the settee, me right behind him.

On the floor, pushed up against the back of the couch is a mattress, pillows piled up and covers disregarded. Two women are there, one sitting on the side of the mattress and the other propped up against the pillows, very pregnant and oh, wow! She's the most beautiful woman I have ever seen. She's got light red hair, all long and curly and messy, and ivory skin covered all over with a mist of freckles. She looks up at Hunter and smiles a smile at him that I'd die to have smiled at me. Hunter sits down beside her, dark skin beside pale, and takes her hand in his and lifts it to his lips like a prince would with his lady.

Then she looks at me. I'm melting! Her eyes have almost no color in the dim light, just a pale, pale hazel that is hardly there at all. I just stand there feeling conspicuous.

'I found him, Puck,' he says to her softly. Then he addresses the older woman, still sitting side-on to me, long fingers stroking stray hairs from the younger woman's slightly sweaty face.

'How far apart?' he asks.

'Still twenty minutes, give or take,' she replies with a deep, earthy voice. 'Long time yet. Maybe the morning,' and she gets up and stretches and walks over to me while Hunter snuggles close into Puck's body.

'Let's have a dram,' as she takes my hand and draws me, staring, round to the settee. She reaches into one of the crates supporting the low table and brings up a good-labeled quart of *uiske beatha*—whisky— and two shot glasses. While she's pouring I continue to stare. Black hair woven into hundreds of braids, tattoos all over her face and hands, earrings hanging from both ears, each different from the other but both looking like they're maybe made of bronze, both with little dark-red and dark-green gemstones winking in the light of the candles. She's wearing a black jumper two sizes too big for her tiny body and a pair of loose ex-army khakis tucked into calf high lace-ups. She's also kinda beautiful, but in a strange way.

She hands me a glass. 'Slànte,' she grins, touching hers to mine, 'I'm Brighid.'

She downs the strong drink in one mouthful and pours another. 'So, I guess you're wondering about all this.'

'God, yes,' I reply, just sipping.

'Well, you're the Rowan, aren't you.' Not a question. 'And you're gonna help us.'

Another moan and the sounds of Hunter guiding Puck's short puffing breaths.

'Time?' calls Brighid.

'Same,' replies Hunter holding up a little clock so that Brighid can check.

She turns back to me. I must look a mess. My nose is running as it thaws out and I try not to be too obvious as I wipe my sleeve over my face. I'm tired to death and feel like an abused dishrag on a comedown as the adrenaline settles from crazy to calm.

Brighid pulls out a wad of tissues from the pocket of her trousers and hands me some.

'I'm sure I'll be crying before this thing's over,' she says, 'but you deserve some. They're clean,' she assures me as I hesitate. I grin sheepishly and turn my head to blow.

'See, the Rowan's got to bear witness.' Full stop. Just that.

'I'm *so* lost,' I say emphatically. 'I've got *no* idea what I'm doing here.'

Right when I'm about to hear the point of this whole weird thing there's the sound of voices, and boots crunching on gravel, coming from the tracks.

I look at Brighid, but she just pats my hands and says, 'It'll wait, don't lose the plot.' And she rises to greet the newcomers. I sigh.

Four more people jump up onto the ledge and come into the room, chattering and laughing, and head straight for the fire dumping an assortment of instruments onto the chairs around them and stripping off coats and hoods and scarves. Three men, one woman.

'Whoosh,' says one guy to Brighid as she pours more shots for the others, 'wee chilly out, ma'am.' Brighid chuckles as the others chatter over each other in excitement.

'It's begun,' she says quietly.

Silence. Another moan from behind the settee. 'Same,' calls Hunter.

Nothing from the others. They just look at Brighid with what looks like wonder in their eyes.

'How was the gig?' asks Brighid, knowing that it really didn't matter to them anymore.

'When?' asks one of the men.

'Bout two hours ago,' she replies. She looks at me and grins, 'but we found the Rowan!'

They all move round and start shaking my hands and slapping me on the back. The girl with them, short, ragged, spiky plum-colored hair, big brown eyes and too much make-up, pushes them aside and holds out her hand for me to shake.

'Rude, aren't they?' she says as she grips my hand like she wants to arm-wrestle. 'I'm called Black Annis.' She tilts her head to the others, 'and this here's Willie and Trev and Matt. We're the band.'

'Oh, yeah, I guessed that,' I say lamely.

'And I'm the harper,' she says proudly, 'and we just played a gig without Puck and we *still* pulled it off." She raises her voice just enough so that Puck could hear. '*Still pulled it off,*' she chortles.

'Don't raise your voice,' calls Hunter.

Black Annis puts one arm through mine and the other through Brighid's and leads us to the sofa where she plops us all down in a heap.

The other guys are hanging some of their instruments on the hooks beside the hose and laying others on the bench. I catch sight of a bodhràn, and Black Anis' harp, but miss seeing the rest.

'As I said, we're the band,' continues Black Annis, 'and we call ourselves *Fianna*, and this here's our manager,' she says, looking at

Brighid who laughs, 'and I gather you've been introduced to Puck and Hunter.'

I don't bother to answer.

'Hah!' she laughs, eager that I seem not to be too upset. 'Hunter's our bodyguard, and all 'round leader you might say.'

'*You* might say,' says Brighid feigning indignation.

'What in God's name is going on here?' I plead, despairing of getting a clear answer from anyone.

'Don't take my name in vain,' I hear from the big man behind the settee, followed by the sounds of Puck in the grip of another contraction.

'Annis, tell him,' says Matt, grinning like a fool, sitting around the other side of the table.

'They're in love, you see?' says Annis. 'Love,' and she snuggles up closer to me.

'It's been a long time,' says Willie, joining us and downing a glass of the *uiske beatha*—whisky.

'Long time,' echoes Matt.

'What?' I feel like the word's become my mantra and I'm stuck with it.

Brighid turns my face to hers. 'No one might know about tonight. No one 'cept you, Rowan. And that'd be wrong.' I wait. Annis snuggles deeper. I like her. She's growing on me.

'See Puck's a human woman, even though she'll never go back.

Not now, 'cause of Hunter, you see? 'Cause of the child. And 'cause she doesn't want to anyway.'

I'm gone. I'm lost. So I just wait.

Puck and Hunter get up from behind the settee. 'I need to move a bit,' says Puck.

Brighid gets up to go to her. 'S'okay, I'm fine,' Puck reassures the older woman.

She gives Hunter a little push away. 'Go sit,' she says to the big man, him pushing the dreadlocks away from his face. 'Make a coffee or something useful. Keep yourself awake.' She smiles.

I can see he doesn't want to be away from her and I wonder at how much he'd borne to come out into the night and find me. And I was still none the wiser as to why. Hunter watches from the arm of the settee as Puck caresses her own belly.

'Hey, hey!' says Annis, turning my face back from the vision that's Puck. 'She's taken.'

'I know that,' I say defensively, looking at Hunter who's looking down at me.

Then he smiles for the first time and it's the biggest, whitest, healthiest set of teeth I've ever seen, only made a little unnerving by the length of the canines.

'I can understand him, Annis,' he says, 'leave the poor boy be.'

'Look me. Look me, Rowan,' says Annis bouncing.

'Okay,' I say grinning at her. 'You're pretty cute for a girl.' She chortles with pleasure. I wonder at how comfortable I'm feeling with these crazies.

I turn back to Brighid. 'Like you were saying?'

'Puck's human.'

I must be looking stupid or something. 'And?' I say, thinking this is all one big joke somehow.

'And we're not,' she replies seriously.

'And you're–?'

'We're the People,' she replies as though I ought to understand.

When it's obvious I don't she says 'The People. The land, you know?' I'm shaking my head, little quick shakes.

Her mouth forms a thin, determined line.

'We're the People. The land. The forests. Wolves and things; ravens and seals and all. All of it. Understand me, Rowan.' She's frowning.

'What,' I smile. 'Like the Little People?'

'Do we look little to you?' says Hunter calmly.

'N-no.'

'But we get called that,' says Trev in my defense.

'You're on the right track,' Willie backs him up.

'You're telling me you're like the Fair Folk out of the legends?' I blurt, getting ready to laugh at the joke.

Puck contracts again, much sooner than the last time. Hunter goes to help her through it.

No one's laughing at the joke. They're all just looking at me.

'This is not fair,' I whine.

Brighid interrupts the beginning of my tirade, 'This is the first time...' She takes a breath, 'This is the *first* time in over a thousand years that a mortal woman's taken one of our kind to love willingly, and a child of the two gets to be born.'

The others smile, great beaming smiles and Annis puts her arms around me and nuzzles my neck.

'And it's the first time since I can remember – and I'm *really* old,

Rowan,' I look at her. Forty maybe? 'And it's the first time since the Quicken got cut down that a child gets born from one of you and one of us at the midwinter solstice.' Tears well up, unshed. She wipes them away furiously.

'And you're the Rowan so you're the witness because the little one brings the magic back into this world,' says Annis softly into my ear.

'So now there's hope,' says Hunter from over near the fire where he holds Puck through a contraction.

'Maybe,' mumbles Brighid."

3

WHEN YOU LOVE SOMEBODY

FOR COVEN

WHEN YOU LOVE SOMEBODY, TRULY LOVE THEM the love is magic because magic is love. You lay no claims, you claim no chains you demand nothing and fear nothing… And fear everything, but that's okay because at least you're feeling something and to feel this much is a lot of responsibility.

When you love somebody you never love just them. You get the family and the clan and the rules they live by even if you hate them. You don't fight them, you don't deny them, you respect love and you give honor to others who have loved them before you, without you and independently of you.

When you love somebody, you'll do everything you can to please them but that's dangerous, the most dangerous thing of all because you just might expect the same back and not everybody can do that. So, you stop, and you ask each other questions but by all that's magic you'll compromise if you truly love and if you truly love you won't lose yourself at all because love is about trust.

When you love somebody, you must trust yourself. It has nothing to do with the beloved. You don't have to trust them, you don't have to anything and that's the point. Sooner or later you're going to hurt each other and that's when that trust in yourself is the trust in love because love does not lie. It can't. Only people lie and when they do—except to protect clan and family from outsiders, who might want to hurt them, and that lying is just plain clever—when people do lie, it's cowardice and no one can love a coward.

When you love somebody, you accept your own freedom, you have nothing to say about that of the beloved. You do not, for a moment, compromise your ideals or your wisdom or your honor or your art because the person who truly loves another person loves that about you and when you change they'll love that too. When you love somebody, you learn to listen when you run out of things to say. You talk about death because one day it's going to happen and it's important to know someone will weep for you because you were loved.

Love allows. Anything else is not love but obligation. When lovers unite their two clans and their two families they bring a whole lot more strength to both because united we stand and there's been enough division in the world.

You owe each other nothing. You are not bound; you have no obligation within this relationship. If you can love each other despite this, if you can trust yourselves to defend this savage freedom then you will stay a distance you never dreamed you could, and steer a course through any wilderness no matter how vast, and when it comes time to let each other go?

Even if it's a suicide pact at a hundred and forty? It'll be with love because love is magic, and magic is eternal, and you'll be there to hold the hand of the beloved and you'll meet them in the air and in the soil, in the river and sacred well, in the mating calls of owls and bears and foxes and wolves, and the wild excitement of hounds and horses as they ready for the hunt.

The freedom of love is the only real love and the only real freedom. If you have that, truly have that you have magic as your garment, the art of living as your sword and every day as a feast upon your table.

4

SPRING EQUINOX

LORE

I LET MY HAND REST GENTLY, REVERENTLY on the *book of spells* my mother has left me. I feel stupid.

Who am I kidding? I think.

The room's a mess. I hadn't bothered to bank up the old slow combustion stove before I'd gone to bed last night so it's as dead as the garden. I walk out onto the porch, sighing, and sit down on the steps with my two mongrels – Jessie and Mate, slow-wagging their tails beside me - and I look out over the dusty morning.

The sunrise is very red. Another bad day.

I wonder, just like everyone else I've talked to, just where the rains have gone. Supposed to come down weeks ago. Weeks.

Nip in the air and the ravens are calling up the day.

If I'm going to try to work the old magic I ought to believe in it – isn't that how it goes?

Cecily did. Everybody trusted her – everybody 'round here, despite whatever they might have thought of us amongst themselves.

No rain. Too long. Winter's near over, and the weatherman can call it El Niño or whatever he likes – it makes us all wonder what summer's going to bring.

No, I think, *better not even contemplate.*

No point planting out the good seed because the way things stand it's all just going to blow away. I pull the blanket tighter around me as the dawn wind raises goose flesh on my arms.

Pretty lonely.

Oh well; nothing for it. Later on today I'll dance the spell. Works or it doesn't.

Just like that, I make up my mind.

'Buena,' I say to the dogs.

It's too early to go to town – might as well get the damned stove started and have a cup of coffee.

I'm just getting up to go inside when I see the dust of a vehicle churning up the road leading to my place. Not expecting anyone, 'specially not at this hour. Me and the dogs wander over towards the gate. The hens hear our footsteps and come 'bock-bocking' out from under the house demanding breakfast.

'Hiss 'em,' I call to the dogs that oblige by running them off 'til I know what's going on.

Yep, coming this way, sure as. Looks like a big old bus.

I'm just leaning on the fence when this thing that looks like it shouldn't be allowed to be on the road pulls into the gate and stops.

Hmm. I figure I ought to be a little wary, but I'd gone and left the shotgun up at the house. The dogs don't seem alarmed – Mate isn't even bothered to stand up while Jessie's got that stupid look she gets when she figures someone's come just to see her.

The door opens. First off, this young guy comes out, lookin' pretty ordinary in jeans and a duffel-coat; clean-shaven, nice open-kinda face, but then this weirdo little woman, no more'n five foot one or two, all covered in tattoos with those long fancy braids like the African women sometimes have (only this woman's white) drops down after him and I look down at the dogs hoping they'll growl a warning or something. Nothing.

The woman takes the lead and comes right on over, bold as brass, and squats down to ruffle the fur around Jessie's neck like she's a little safe pet or something when she looks as much like a big old wolf as you'd ever want to see. Stupid dog's rolling on her back.

'Beautiful morning,' she says to me, looking up.

'Whatever,' I answer coolly. 'Can I help you?'

'We're on tour,' pipes up the guy, walking over to me with his hand held out. 'Name's Rowan.' I shake his hand with what I hope's a challenging grip.

'What are you, a rock band or somethin'?' I ask, looking at the bus and figuring they couldn't be very successful at it.

'Rocked-up folk,' she says, standing up.

'Just you two?' I eye the bus again.

'The others are still sleeping,' she replies. 'There's nine of us."

Alarm bells.

'You're a long way outa town,' I say frankly, 'you need directions or somethin'?'

'We've just come from there,' says Rowan, 'everything's still shut up. No motel.'

'Small town,' I reply.

'We were wondering if you could maybe put us up out here?' he asks.

I guess I must be looking like I'm dumb or struck deaf. 'Sir?' he asks again.

I laugh. 'You're kidding, right?' I say.

'We wouldn't get in your way or anything,' says the woman. 'Oh, sorry, my name's Brighid by the way.'

She holds out this little hand all covered in intricate spirals and triscele tattoos for me to shake. What can I do? So, I shake her hand and it's surprisingly firm – not forced either.

'We could help out a bit 'til we get paid for some gigs – then we could pay our way,' she adds enthusiastically.

I gesture around me at the old house and barn and utilities sheds. All had seen seriously better days but probably long before I was born.

'Do I look like I've got room for guests?' I try to keep a straight face.

'Something about the place,' says Brighid. 'I felt it from the road. It's a good place.'

'Been better,' I shrug. 'You some kinda mystic, lady?' I ask sarcastically. Then she smiles at me and *'oh my,'* darts, like a swallow, through my mind.

'Some kind, yeah,' she replies.

Whatever.

'Look,' I say, 'it's early. You can come on up to the house if you want and I can make us some coffee and I'll see if I can think.'

That smile again.

We wander back over to the house, assaulted by the hens on the way. I excuse myself for just a minute and grab the feed box from the porch to keep the girls quiet. Rowan and Brighid just stand there waiting 'til I come back.

We walk on into my house and I'm really embarrassed at the mess, but I figure that once I get the fire started and the percolator on I'll give it a quick going over. Doesn't really matter I suppose – it's not like I'm entertaining or anything – but Cecily would have been disgusted with me.

'Scuse the state of the place,' I say, moving books, more books, my writing things and my notebooks, off the couch and dumping them on the floor beside. 'Sit if you feel like it.'

Brighid comes over to me, 'You get the coffee sorted and I'll light the stove, okay?'

'It's a bitch of a thing, lady.' I answer.

'I'm good with a fire,' she replies with a something in her eyes. She squats down and starts stacking the kindling in a neat little criss-cross in the grate.

'Suit yourself,' I say, impressed.

I pull three mugs down from the cupboard along with the canister in which I keep my good Italian coffee – my pleasure, you know? – and I measure out enough for that perfect first brew of the day. 'You take milk and sugar?' I ask over my shoulder.

'Yeah, two and milk,' replies Rowan.

'No,' says Brighid, 'neat's perfect.'

'You read all this stuff?'

I turn back to Rowan who's stacking my books in a tidy pile, looking at the titles as he does so.

'Yeah,' I reply defensively. Nobody 'round here's interested in my passion – history, mythology, the supernatural and the like. I stopped trying to talk about it with anybody years ago.

'Hmm,' says Rowan, looking at one in particular – the one on Fionn McCumhail called *The Master of Earth and Water.*"

'I've read this one,' he says, smiling. 'Like it a lot.

Huh?' I think, surprised.

'What's your name?' Brighid asks me.

'Jack Forester, ma'am,' I tell her.

'Grr. How about *Jack Forester, Brighid*,' she says, lifting an eyebrow, eyes as pale as mist, almost white. 'How long you lived here, Jack?'

'All my life, Brighid. Lived here with my mother 'til she died a few years ago.'

'On your own?' she continues.

'Got the dogs,' I reply, thinking *This is none of your business, lady.*

'Just the two of you was there?'

Here I go. I'm not about to talk about this with them. Always people had things to say about Cecily's never having been married and all. Calling me a bastard when I went to school – that and other bad things – 'til I stopped going and started learning from home when the chores were done. Not going to. Loved her *so* much. So I don't answer.

Fire's going strong. Good fire. I lift the iron plate off the stove and put the percolator on and set to shoving mess into the corners out of the way and straightening the covers on the other couch over under the window that I use for a bed. Couldn't be bothered with the bedrooms, me, easier just to live in one room.

Shit. I realize, seeing that I'd left the *book of spells* wide open in plain sight on the covers of my bed. I grab it up and kinda sidle out of the room and down the hallway leading to the bedrooms and the bathroom (for what it was) and open the closet door where I shove it way back on the top shelf.

When I come back into the living room Brighid's already poured the steaming coffee into the mugs. She hands me one, then Rowan, then squats down beside the stove, keeping warm.

'Hi,' I hear from the porch.

Rowan grins and gets up, stumbling over his own feet, calling, 'In here.'

In walks this punky kinda girl with her hair all done up in parrot-colored ties, sticking out every which way, dressed all in black, stomping through the doorway in boots that shoulda been on a man's feet. Rowan gets to her and puts his arms around her and she snuggles into him like they're used to the fit of each other.

This makes three, I think to myself. Another sigh.

'Grab some coffee if you want, love,' I say to her as they come over near the fire. She does.

Rowan sits back down and picks up another book that he'd been flipping through before the parrot-girl came in. 'Wouldn't mind borrowing this,' he says. It's one of my books on local lore about ghosts and hauntings.

I'm not about to let any of my books go into the hands of some stranger so I don't answer.

'I can smell it on you,' says the parrot-girl cryptically. I blush and scowl and wonder if living out here alone for so long hasn't had its effect.

'Shh,' hisses Brighid, 'don't be so quick, Annis,' as Rowan clamps a hand over her mouth. She giggles at him, squirming.

'I apologize if I'm offending you,' I add in my own defense, 'but it's not as though I'd invited any of you.'

Jessie bellies over to me, momentarily leaving Brighid's lap, and I crouch down to stroke her tawny red coat, wishing they'd all just go away.

'Jack, this is Annis,' says Brighid, 'and she's got a mouth, as you'll find out the longer you know her, but she means no harm. She doesn't mean you *smell*, smell.'

'What then?'

'Little magics,' says Annis, 'there's little magics all over you Jack.'

'Don't know what you're on girl,' I imply, 'but you better not be bringing any o' that stuff onto my property.' I drain my cup. 'So now, I've got a lot to do – so if you'd all–'

What's that? *Thunk, thunk, schruuuch* from outside.

What the… I get up and head for the door knowing, just knowing, that one or more of the others from the bus are mucking around my place.

I bolt over the porch and down the steps looking around for them. Can't see 'em. Then I hear it again *thunk, thunk*. The others are behind me.

The noise is coming from my garden patch. I stride 'round the side of the house and there, in what ought to be my early spring vegetable and herb garden, is this huge black guy, stripped to the waist, dreadlocks all tied up on top of his head, darker tattoos than his skin all wavering like serpents over his big-muscled body. He's mattocking up the beds, while another guy – fair skin, long flame-colored hair tied in two plaits, more tattoos – just goes along behind him with my rake, smoothing out what the big guy's turned over.

'What do you think you're *doing?*' I yell. Oh, look, there's more of 'em sitting on the ground inside the fence that keeps the beasts from my patch – two men, a very attractive young woman and a – a baby at her breast. *Oh Mother,* I think, *now what?*

The big guy and the red-haired guy are already sweating despite the sun just up and the nip in the air.

'Turning your ground,' says the big guy seriously.

'Smoko,' says the other pulling a pouch of makings out of the pocket of his jeans as he ambles over to the others.

I'm fuming. Who do they think they are? They would've had to have rummaged in my own barn for the mattock and the rake.

Crowded. They've got me crowded – bloody nerve!

Bunch of strung-out city weirdos, I'm thinking as I gauge the odds. Doesn't matter if they kill me, I'm not going down meek. This is *my* place.

'Get out. Get out the lot of you,' I yell, turning from the three behind me to the others over the fence.

The big guy shoulders the mattock and comes towards me, looking straight at me with the blackest eyes I've seen outside of an animal.

He opens the gate and comes over, lowers the mattock and leans on the handle (and I thought I was tall). 'Can't do that,' he says straight.

'Wh-what?' I say stupidly, dead-scared as he looms over me. Nope. Won't be put down.

'I want you all to get back on the bus and leave,' I say emphatically.

'Can't,' he replies quietly.

I'm dumbfounded. 'Why not?'

'You're not ready,' he replies.

'For *what*,' I say.

'For the rain,' says Brighid coming to stand beside me and looking up at me with those eyes. 'You're not ready for the rain, Jack.'

I look into those pale silver-grey eyes wishing I'd known her when I was a younger man; wishing she didn't look quite so strange, anyway; wishing she'd come alone.

'I was,' I stop myself sharply. *What am I doing?* I was just about to blab about doing the spell.

'Look around you, woman,' I say. 'Does it bloody-well look like rain to you?'

'It'll rain,' says the big guy, rubbing his hands on his army surplus pants and holding one out for me to shake. 'I'm Hunter. The guy with the rake's Willie, the lady's name's Puck and our son's Robin. The lazy guys are Matt and Trevor.'

I shake his hand unwillingly. Not a shred of threat reaches me from any of them.

'Jack,' I say.

'Figures,' he replies. He reaches up and undoes the cord that's keeping his dreads back and they fall around him like live things – looks like he's got about two dozen black-bird feathers mixed in with them.

'You really ought to loosen up, Jack,' he says. 'Can I grab a drink of water or something – throat's pretty dry already.'

This whole thing's got me mind-rackingly confused, so what's this little bubble of excitement – this little thread of real pleasure – that's kinda sneaking up on me? Things around here are desperate. I must be loco to be even considering having them stay awhile.

Later on that morning I pick up the keys off the hook inside the barn and *yee-up* the dogs onto the flatbed of the truck.

Hunter's back in the patch working it hard, like it's his own, and his lady, what's her name? Oh yeah, Puck – well Puck, along with the other two guys, are up at the house fixing up a stack of food. From their own supplies.

I've got to go into town and organize water deliveries to come and fill up my near-depleted tanks. Doesn't matter if these people think rain's coming, I'm not risking it.

I crank over the engine when Rowan yells 'Wait up,' from the porch. He comes running across the yard asking if I'm going into town. When I tell him yeah, he asks if some of them can get a ride in with me to see about supplies and to maybe set up a gig somewhere.

'Won't be long,' he says, going off to get the others.

He comes back with Annis and Brighid and Matt and Willie. Brighid and Willie pull themselves up into the cab with me and the others hop up onto the tray along with the dogs.

We're driving along causing a sky full of dust behind us and Willie pulls out this little tin whistle from his pocket and starts playing a reel. Brighid keeps looking at me and grinning. Must admit by the time we get into town I'm smiling to myself and tapping on the wheel like a kid.

I stop the truck outside of Blake's Farm Supplies to the startled faces of two local women sitting on the seat out front. Brighid comes with me while the others go off to the pub to try to convince the proprietor into letting them play there.

Inside Tom Blake's telling Marty Swain that the water deliveries are backed up until after the weekend. I wait, resigned to the same story. Brighid's got her arm hooked through mine, and I'm feeling pretty good about that when Tom and Marty look up from the order book. They see me standing there with Brighid and I figure I know what they're thinking but by now that warm bubble I felt in the truck has spread out through my whole self and I just don't care. They're not about to say anything to my face anyway – country folk always wait 'til you're not around.

'Morning Tom,' I say casually. 'Three days you say for the tankers?'

'Ah, yeah, Jack.' He clears his throat. 'You ordering?'

'Tsk,' whispers Brighid quietly.

'What?' I say looking down at her.

'Nothing, Jack. Doesn't matter,' she replies sighing.

'Put me down to get both my tanks filled up, will you Tom? Got company for a while.'

Tom looks at me like I'm a fool, shrugs and pushes his glasses up his nose and writes up the order. Marty's staring at Brighid then smirking at me. Tom's mumbling under his breath.

'Anything else?' he asks dryly. *Yeah, fuck you too, Tom*, I'm thinking.

'Just the water thanks Tom,' I say, turning us towards the door.

'Monday, Jack,' he replies.

'Whatever, Tom,' and I pull the door shut deliberately without slamming it.

My jaw's all clenching and unclenching. Brighid stops us and looks at me.

'Someplace we can sit and drink something cold while we wait for the others?' She's tactful; I'll say that for her.

We walk over to the cafe, take a couple of chairs at a table and I order us cold apple juices from the waitress. She's smiling at Brighid who's smiling back.

When she's gone Brighid turns to me and takes both my hands in her own. 'Been hard has it, Jack?' she asks.

'Don't wanna talk about it,' I say.

'Annis is right, Jack. There's little magics all around you. And the things you read? Humph. Seems to me you don't fit the picture you're trying so hard to fit.' Eyes as soft as dawn on a pond, she's got. I just sort of start talking.

'Mother's name was Cecily,' I say. 'Came here with me in her belly already, and started out renting that house I live in now. Don't know how she managed at first nor who was there, if anyone, when I was born. When I was older she told me that first off people weren't too nice. I always called her Cecily, too, by the way – never knew her as anything else.

'But she had the gift you see? Planted out herbs and made tonics and potions and poultices for every which thing, and she could find underground water anywhere 'cept our place with these two bent up old wire coat hangers. Had this pack of cards and people'd come and she'd shoo me off to play while she'd tell 'em things private.

'Even as early as I can remember there was always somebody coming or going. Thing was, no one ever hung around. All she really had, people-wise, was me. When she wasn't busy she would read to me or else teach me about the stuff in the garden. Some nights she'd take me walking way off from the house and we'd lie on the ground on our backs while she pointed out what group of stars meant what. I loved that.'

The waitress brings the juices and I pay then and there. Brighid keeps hold of one of my hands.

'Was when I went to school that the trouble started,' I continue when we're by ourselves again, unable to shut up like Brighid has cast some kind of enchantment on me or something.

'Kids'd call me a bastard and go on and on about me not having a father; call Cecilly a slut and a witch like it was a dirty word. First fight I was only six – they kept happening 'til Cecilly took me out of school a year later. The school never did send any authorities 'round to make me go back.

'I'd asked her about a dad, but she wouldn't go there. *"He was just a man,"* she'd say dismissively without meaning to hurt my feelings. I'd ask her about being a witch. She'd laughed at that and said, *"Whatever."*

'So, in the end I'd do my chores and Cecily would teach me,

always bringing home dozens of books from the library and I really liked it 'cause she was always so happy and excited about the stuff – it was like we were exploring the world together. It was her'd loved the history and the myths and stuff – passed the passion on, I suppose.'

'What did she look like Jack?' asked Brighid.

'Oh, long dark brown hair smelling of the garden.' I recall, as the memory of her when she was younger rose up so strongly she might have been just a mist away.

'She had strange eyes though, always changing color with her moods. She was short too Brighid, just a tad taller than you. She used to let her hair hang loose mostly 'though occasionally she'd tuck it all up under a cap when she had a lot of manual work to do. And strong. Never seeming to need anyone.' I paused, thinking.

'She died from pneumonia. Got real sick that deep cold winter three years back. I did all the right tisanes just like she'd showed me, but she just got worse. I even went so far as to ask her if I could get in the doctor, maybe get those antibiotics into her. She wouldn't have it. *"Time I died,"* she'd said. And she did.

'When I was straightening away her stuff after I'd got her buried.'

Brighid interrupted me. 'Where's she buried Jack?'

I smiled as I recalled. 'A few miles south of here the land climbs into the hills. We went there lots once we'd discovered it. Deep in there's this big wall of stone maybe twenty-foot-high kinda up on its end. We'd always go there. Cecily never had a problem leaving the set paths to go searching for the wild herbs as they're always best. Right near that stone there's a pool that we used to cool our feet in on the hot days. It was spring-fed and never seemed to me to have a bottom.

Wouldn't swim there. Buried her there.

'Anyway, when I was straightening up all her stuff, packing away most of it, I found a big old box that she had hidden away in back of the wardrobe. It had a lot of her memories in it. Photos of people I didn't know – old photos, some *really* old. Some old jewelry, the deed for the farm – never knew when, let alone how, she'd managed that. Never realised that we owned the place, and...'

I pause to look at Brighid. *Why not?* I say to myself.

'And a book of spells.' Her eyebrows go up but that's about all. 'And a letter that said *Jack* on the envelope.

'I remember that I was afraid to open that letter, don't know to this day why. I left it on the kitchen table for a whole week before I read it. I was angry for months after – and scared that maybe she'd been crazy all along and that I hadn't known it because I didn't know any better.

'In the letter she told me that she loved me and always would; that I wasn't supposed to get the letter 'til after she'd died in case I wouldn't love her anymore. Felt it was important, blah blah. She wrote in it that my father hadn't been a human; that she'd loved him but that he lived in an entirely other world and that he couldn't cross between like she could and that he'd been sad that he could never touch me or know me – his own child – and that she'd have to do all his loving and teaching *for* him. Said he was a man of the sídhe. Said he'd told her that someday he'd find a way.'

I stopped when Brighid took a huge deep breath. I'm rambling. 'Sorry,' I say.

She's been looking down all throughout. She looks up now and her eyes are as smiling as her mouth, 'That answers that then, doesn't it?' she says and kisses me fair on the lips.

I feel the blood rush to my face. And it's like perfect timing or something because the others have spotted us and are whooping and hollering on their way over to the table.

'Got it,' says Annis, all grins.

'Me too,' says Brighid. I'm about to ask her what she means when we all hear it. Distant thunder.

Rowan joins us a few minutes later, all loaded with fresh supplies. We pile ourselves and the rest into the truck just as the strong smell of ozone wafts on the rising breeze.

It starts raining on the drive home.

5

A SELKIE LOVE STORY

LORE

HE SAT ON THE CLOSEST ROCK, with the cold black water and white, lace-like froth shushing at his edges; his boots, his tiny rubber currach held onto, without thinking, by its rope. He watched me with some emotion, some edges of both passion and panic that made no sense to me then, with eyes that were the dark brown of a distant relative and that told me of his soul.

Alright, I thought at him. *I'll play with you, I have to, so do not look away.*

And he did not so I suppose he heard me thinking.

I was slow for him, reaching up and pulling my face away. That first rush of air on my other skin caught my breath and it was I, not he, who shuddered with surprise. He did not drop his gaze from mine even then, as if to say, *I'm with you, don't be afraid.*

I give love for that, for he should have been in dread, if the stories were true.

Then down my neck I rolled it, over one shoulder, over the other. Pulled it to below both breasts, enticing. His eyes widened, and his nostrils did this little thing and I knew why. He looked upon the milk white skin of a woman wherever the silk of my silver pelt peeled away.

His breath came faster, deeper, because he knew what I was and what I could do and what was to come and what I would give and that I would leave him and all of it I read in his eyes with their deep black centers that grew wider until the rim had all but been pushed aside.

No one he knew had ever seen this, he told me later, only told of it as though it might just have once been real, him covering my freezing flesh with his arms, knowing my pelt would consign the chill into memory as soon as I clothed my body within. After this. What a gentle man he turned out to be.

How could I have resisted? He'd stood in those great boots, that thick woolen jacket covered by a sou'wester that stood out like a sail in the wind, smelling of the fish of days gone by, his jeans filthy where he'd rubbed his hands on them after gutting.

He dropped the rope to his little boat.

Then it was me who could not look away. We'd fished this same wild sea garden for generations and we'd seen each other a hundred times or perhaps a hundred more and we had so much love to give each other, and I was ripe, and I didn't question that it was to be him.

I pushed the pelt down, down over my hips and knees. And not even to kill him or to do any of the things my mother and her mother had told me that I could do. And why would I? No, just to lie with him and love him.

I step from one skin only to expose another, all the way and I let it all go, and I let his eyes wander before I took hold of him to touch his roughness and pull him further from the water.

You just going to leave it? he whispered, pulling his gloves off and reaching around my shoulders with his salt stiff jacketed arms, but with hands as careful as could be. As if it, my true nature, would go off on its own. Why would he think that? And there was no one else and the cliff was his. I knew the stories, so I had no fear.

We followed the grooves in the sand into the little shelter that kept the wind away and that smelled of things I would never need the words for. And then he laid me down on his big woollen coat and he kissed my lips and he explored my woman body, and then he entered me and oh, that was that, so I knew what a man was and what he did, and what a woman could feel, and it was wordless, achingly wordless, and then he wrapped me in the coat and we lay together with just the sounds of the wind and the sea and the gulls up on the cliffs.

Eventually I sighed, and stood, and pulled him, frowning, from the floor, and he was sad. It was sad, but I could never have stayed.

And unlike the other stories he walked me to the water's edge, took back his coat, and watched and shivered and cried just a little when I stepped into my skin again.

I took to the black water, his child within me, and I saw him every day that he came and we all shared the same wild sea garden as long as he is alive. And he knew.

6

MIDSUMMER SOLSTICE

LORE

THE BUS CHUGS OVER THE CREST OF THE hill and we look down over the splendor of the bay.

'What a vision,' I whisper to Hunter.

I slow the bus enough to drink in the sight. The sea in the distance is all whitecaps and dark blue water leading onto a long crescent of beach, the town right down close to the shore. The bay curves around like a big U; the hills hung with morning mist off to the left and the headland to the right dotted with all the headstones reflecting the early sunlight where the salt-spray had damped them during the night.

I crank the bus into low gear for the steep decline as a two-train semi barrels past me in the outside lane causing the bus to take a sideways lurch towards the guard rail. *Hate those things,* I think.

Hunter's up front with me, with Robin belted into his lap playing some kind of finger game. The others are down back.

'Hey, come take a look,' I yell, and they all crowd up close for the big panorama.

'How you doing, Willie?' asks Jack. 'Is it far now or do you want me to take the wheel for a while.'

'Nah, be there in ten minutes as the crow flies,' I reply grinning. Hunter chuckles at me as he passes Robin back to whoever will take him. He stretches in the seat.

'Home,' he says softly.

The forest out back of the bay is the place of the Summer Gathering. A whole year's been spent in some shitty, lousy destinations, playing some good gigs and some terrible, gathering the Lost along the way.

We found three of the Lost people this year: Rowan and Jack and Gypsy. Rowan and Black Annis (she's the one Jack insists on calling Parrot Girl even though she's changed the color of her hair maybe five times since he met her. It's pink for the Gathering) are an item. Jack still hasn't made the move on Brighid, though I'm not surprised - she's a pretty formidable babe.

And Gypsy? She worked at the cafe in the town near where we stayed last. Brighid had met her for just a brief moment the first morning in the town but she hadn't picked her 'cause she'd apparently been distracted by Jack at the time. We noticed her at the gig that night though. She'd been up front, dancing through every set, ice-white hair flying around her head as she let loose. Couldn't miss her really, she was the only person in the pub game enough to get on the dance floor.

Turns out she'd been a blow-in from the city and had landed the waitress job right off as the woman before her had only just left to have a baby. You wouldn't think to look at her that she'd be so deep down dark angry. Happens a lot, though, when the magic's strong in a person. They never do fit in with the surface world.

I cruise the bus down the main street of town. The sidewalks on both sides of the road are already crowded with tourists. Can spot a few of the Folk amongst them ad it seems more are out and about than last year.

It's a little easier here than most places we go. There's so many rainbow people and hippies and mystics, musicians and dreamers already live here or else in the hills around the bay that the authorities don't pay us too much attention. We occasionally get searched for dope or guns. Either that or they try to find something to give us a hard time over, but it's not like some places.

Jack's right up behind me leaning on the back of mine and Hunter's seats staring and mumbling as he takes it all in. We got a bumper crop out of his patch while we were at his place and there was a bit of a frenzy getting all the medicinals ground and pounded and steeped and bottled and jarred but we've got a pretty impressive load of lotions and potions on board, enough to share out at the gathering, and plenty of still-fresh produce so we won't have to buy much, if anything. Trevor stayed behind there, this year, to keep the place going. He loves chickens and they took to him like Jack didn't exist anymore. Got to find ourselves another bodhràn player though. Still, I figure there'll be a stray or two at the fair.

Out the other side of town a way and we turn off onto the dirt track. We follow behind a big old blue car that's loaded with the Folk. They're leaning out the windows calling and laughing as we eat their dust. *That's okay,* I think to myself, *you'll wait.*

Hunter reaches over and pulls one of my plaits. 'I can hear you thinking, Willie. Be nice,' he grins. I smile back, sure of myself.

The battle of champions takes place every year at the Gathering and I've been training hard, doing the run to town from Jack's place over the roughest terrain I could find, and fighting with Hunter who's really my only challenge amongst the band members.

The battle has got three categories: the run, the one-on-one staff fight and the best filíocht. For the last three years Sheila ní Dubh has won the best poet and I'm nowhere near her league, and as far back as anyone can remember no one's ever beaten Hunter with the staff but I intend to make a good second. The run's up for grabs.

I slow down as we pass through the wide gate and rattle over the cattle-grid on the last leg of the journey, and drive along a couple of hundred yards to where the forest opens out onto a huge clearing. Not many here yet so we get to pick a good spot to park the bus. I maneuver the thing into a pocket of deep shade 'cause by the time the sun gets to mid-morning it's going to be a scorcher.

Robert and Shauna, the custodians of this place, see us from where they're helping some guys to put up the big main marquee and come slowly over to greet us.

'Robert's looking old,' I say to Hunter as we set up camp, the others of the band bringing bits and pieces out of the bus.

Mate and Jessie start barking a warning, but Hunter looks in the dogs' direction. That shuts them up.

Robert's an O'Neill and Shauna's his good wife. His ancestors have been settled in this area since the time of the first crossing when most of us left the homeland due to the troubles. An O'Neill, way back, decided that none of the family would partake of the Quicken Brew and none of them, to my knowledge, ever have. They've lived and died quite contentedly, passing down the generations the task of hosting the Gatherings – and keeping the secret.

They never get too personal with any of us. That's to save us the sadness, I figure. Love them for it.

Robert comes up to Hunter and does his little bow thing, just like they always do, saying 'Fáilte, Milord', and they go off together to talk the news of the area so that Hunter can pass on anything significant to the rest of us and we can get word out if there's likely to be trouble.

Cars and vans keep coming all morning. People're erecting shelters and stalls to sell their stuff or whatever, and making little homes all over the clearing. I had to laugh, I suppose, when Rowan said to me *"They just look like anybody else only weirder,"* as though he was expecting us to be the only normal-looking ones.

Today's just for setting up and playing music and getting to know each other again, for hearing the tales of the journeys and for meeting the special people that we've gathered along the way and who are prepared to work in with us. To find out which of them will take the Quicken Brew, once they know the danger.

Puck and Rowan and Gypsy and Jack have already been told.

Jack's not sure he wants that kind of responsibility, even feeling like he does for Brighid. There's no way that Puck's not going to partake 'cause like she and Hunter aren't going to love each other as far into the future as I can imagine. Rowan and Gypsy are in for the long ride, they've said already.

Oh, about Jack. When Robin was born we'd been sure he'd been the first of the half-kind. Hadn't known there'd been some rogue fairy out there making out with a witch in the backwater.

Brighid hates it when I use the 'f' word. Can never get over the joke though, about having little wings and all. Cried myself to sleep the first time I heard what they'd turned us into for the sake of killing us off in people's minds. What? Did some freak figure we'd just go away after that? Still, got so I could see the funny side.

Hunter strides over to us looking grim. He sits down on the ground indicating for the rest of us to join him. There's a dark haze of worry all around him. He indicates for Brighid to sit to his left and Puck to his right. *Oh, oh,* I think, as the rest of us sit.

'Would you three mind not staying?' he asks, looking first at Gypsy, then Rowan, then Jack. *Uh, oh,* I think again, more and more alert. They leave us goodheartedly enough, but I can hear them wondering.

'There's been a fire,' Hunter begins. 'Kate O'Neill and her husband and their kids.' Alarm bells.

'Bad?' asks Brighid, shock registering on her face.

'All dead,' replies Hunter.

'But what about—' I begin.

'Stop,' says Hunter, 'I've got more.' We wait. 'Looks like it was deliberate.'

Confusion.

'*Why?*' asks Puck.

'Robert and Shauna are destroyed,' continues Hunter, his voice dark, his eyes like black coals as he looks around at all of us.

The penny drops. Kate and her children were the only living descendants of this branch of the O'Neills. The Guardians. Robert and Shauna are too old to take the Quicken Brew, it'd kill 'em even before their time.

End of the line.

'Who'd *do* this?' says Brighid.

'Well it's not because of the secret unless that husband of hers let it out,' says Hunter.

'Did he know?' asks Puck, not fully up-to-date on the subject.

'He had to know. Kate's job is to raise the kids up to take it on willingly. Kate's brought them to every Gathering since they were born to get used to us. Owen never came but he would've known. Robert's figured he's been trouble all along. Too fond of the drink. Always been a worry.'

Brighid's in tears. 'They were just babies,' she whispers. Kate's children were three and five years old this turning of the wheel.

'Well right now whoever did this thing is still a mystery. Robert says the cops haven't got a clue. There were petrol drums that didn't belong there dumped at the scene and they've been sent off for DNA tests,' continued Hunter.

Silence.

'The Gatherings,' says Matt.

'We'll have to wait 'til everyone's arrived,' says Hunter. 'Rowan and the others don't need to have their heads confused with any of this, okay? They need to be really calm for the ceremony. No one's to upset them, understood?' We all agree.

I just sit there thunderstruck. If we can't have the Gatherings, we'll be lost again. It took us hundreds of years to get over the inquisition. They were the worst years ever since the Christians took the old ways away from the land in the first place. Some of us died from the terror – the deepest sadness and despair is the only thing that can eventually destroy the sídhe.

I shake myself. *Don't go there,* I think, coming out of that memory as quick as possible. Someone'll figure something out. Right now I need a run. A long run.

Hunter's nowhere.

I've been around all the fires asking after him. And where's Brighid?

The Folk all gathered late afternoon to talk about the problem. Robert had been asked to attend and he'd filled in a few gaps that he hadn't told Hunter earlier, one of which was that the cops hadn't been sure if Owen, Kate's husband, had even been in the house at the time. The house was over a hundred years old, two-story wooden place that's gone up like matchsticks. The bodies inside weren't recognizable when forensics turned up. They'd been sure of the remains of Kate and the kids but if Owen *had* been there it's possible he'd been in a different part of the house and had been incinerated. If he hadn't? Well, no one's seen him since.

The meeting had broken up when the first of the festival bonfires was due to be lit to mark the opening of the gathering.

It was dusk.

There'd been no resolution.

Everybody had lightened up once the first Fire was lit – we had two more days to think of a solution and Robert, after all, could live for several more Gatherings so no one seemed to think the dilemma was an immediate threat.

Bands had played into the night and people had danced and feasted and abandoned themselves to each other. Matt came up with a temporary bodhràn player named Alan who was one of the Lost and hadn't got a foot in the door with any of the established bands. He'd been busting to play. Alan's a great guy, been playing with folk bands up and down the west coast for years now, never settling, as is common.

Fianna played the last set of the night and we rocked the house (as we do!). There was me on fiddle, Matt on the uilleann pipes and both the low whistle and the high whistle, Annis moved between accordion and the harp and backed up Puck, who does guitar, on vocals and, of course, Alan on the bodhràn.

We'd packed up and were having a dram. Puck had taken Robin back from Rowan who'd been dancing him in his arms for most of the night, and had gone off looking for Hunter.

She hadn't found him, nor Brighid either.

What's going on?

'If he doesn't want to be found,' says Puck, 'then he won't be found – you know that Willie.'

Still, it's strange for him to go off and not say a word to anyone.

'Yeah, I know it, Puck got a weird feeling, is all,' I think to myself, not wanting to worry her unduly.

Jack comes over to where we're sitting 'round the hearth-fire next to the bus.

'I found Brighid,' he begins, 'but she wants to be left alone to be with the land. She said Hunter borrowed Hugh Taylor's car and took off while the bands were playing.'

Such a very weird feeling.

'I'm going to find him.' I say, standing. Puck's looking at me, her look loaded with unspoken concern.

'You heard what Puck said,' pipes up Annis.

'Don't care.' No argument.

The last car in was John Finch's. His band's camped right near the track so I go over and ask if I can use his wheels for a while.

'Well I'm not going anywhere,' he slurs, several Guinness's the merrier. 'Keys are in it,' and he returns his attention to his companions.

I've got a gut feeling he's gone out to Kate's place. It's a half-hour drive from when I leave the track and get on the main road. I drive.

I park the car on the track side of the police cordon tape and pass under it and up to the mess. All that's left is the chimney, a lot of cold blackened timber, ash and iron roofing that's scattered around.

The garden shed's still standing though. I've got to fight not to lose it, but my eyes are stinging.

The place stinks. Fear, horror, something unclean I can't quite get — but I can also smell that Hunter's been here already, and gone.

My heart's beating in my throat. Something very bad has happened here — that's the unclean thing that's up my nose. It's worse closer to the shed.

Sit. Touch the earth. Don't know what it was other than the fire. Something. I get myself calm.

Where's Hunter, I summon.

'HEADLAND,' I hear it as quick as that.

'*Beannachta,*' Blessings—I say aloud to the earth and the forest around me.

The moon's high overhead, near full. Wind's soft off the ocean as I walk along the cliff-edge with the buried dead to my right.

I see the silhouette of Hunter's bulk right over at the furthest point of the headland. I wander over, fox-wary, and sit down beside him as casually as I can, knowing that my interference could easily backfire.

I look out of the corner of my eye and can see his jaw clench and unclench. I don't want to initiate a conversation with him – known him a long time and when the dark man gets dark you don't push him. And it's been a while since I've sensed him this dark.

Eventually he rolls his head around to loosen up some stiffness. He's still looking out to sea.

'It was him,' he says softly.

'Who?' I ask.

'Owen,' he answers.

'You sure?'

'Dead sure,' he replies.

'What happens now?' I ask, already knowing where this is going.

'These people have been our allies – our friends – all the way back,' he says very quietly.

He stretches and stands and holds out a hand to pull me up.

'First we're gonna celebrate the Turning,' he says, 'and then I'm going to find him.

'We get back to the camp and you tell Black Annis I got his things outa the shed. Tell her I want a word. I need to be with Puck right now,' and he strides off towards the carpark.

Uh, oh, I think.

As if I didn't know.

Daybreak and there's a knock on the side of the bus that wakes everybody with its insistence. Annis goes and opens it. It's Shauna.

'Sorry to wake you,' she says, 'but it's important. It's Robert.'

Can you wait a minute Shauna,' calls Hunter, pulling on his jeans.

'I'll be lighting your hearth-fire then, Milord,' she calls. Annis chortles at the title.

Shauna's sitting beside a stoic-looking Robert who's got his hands clamped together in his lap, sitting up straight and dressed like he's going to court. The fire's burning brightly and Shauna's put a kettle on to boil.

Robin crawls over to Rowan, his current favorite, and Rowan proceeds to distract him.

Puck sits down beside Hunter and Robert stands.

'I have something to say to you all,' he stutters, looking down at his feet. 'Relax Robert,' says Shauna.

'Yeah chill, Robert,' pipes Annis.

'We want to take the Quicken berry brew,' says Robert.

'You–' begins Hunter.

'I'm sorry to interrupt you Hunter, but please,' whispers Robert.

'Please hear him out, Milord,' says Shauna, 'we've discussed this at great length and have already made plans.'

"I'm listening,' Hunter replies gravely.

'I've made up my mind,' he begins. 'All of you have been our blessing right back to when we were high kings and beyond. A branch of the O'Neills have always guarded the secret, and since the crossing it's been our honor, no our *life*, to keep a piece of the land sacred for both our people.

'Now all that's in jeopardy and me and mine,' he looks lovingly at Shauna, 'have got two choices… And bear it in mind that we're going to die anyway without the second choice.

'First choice is to maybe have a few seasons left and then we die, with no O'Neill to keep the pact.' Shauna cries softly into her handkerchief.

'Second choice is to take the sacred brew, despite the risk, because then we'd get the longevity we'd need to keep the lands for the Gatherings just like we always have. We can deal with the curious when we don't get any older when the time comes. Nobody takes much notice of old people anyway. Shauna won't let me do it without her, just in case I up and die on her.' He looks at all the silent faces.

'And I've covered all the possible problems.' He smiles at Hunter.

'Go on,' says Hunter.

'I've booked Shauna and me on a flight to the old country already. We're due to get on the plane the day after the Gathering folds down.

'If we die from the potion then we want you to just bury us here, where we love – no fuss. If we live we'll take the holiday anyway. One way or the other the authorities won't know anything. We went to town yesterday and mentioned the trip to a few key locals. We told them that we're taking an extended tour and that we'd no idea when we'd be back. And due to our recent tragedy people understand our need to get away.

'We told them that we've had the title of the place put in a distant niece's name.' He nods at Puck, 'In case we decide to stay there.'

'What are you doing, Robert,' asks Puck.

'You're the only one we know amongst the Folk who's like us. You've got a past and you were the only one of the Lost that we know well enough to write out details on the transfer,' he continues. 'Authorities'd check up on any of the rest of you and find out you've got no past, no records that'd stand up under scrutiny. That could be trouble for you.'

'I'm taking the brew tonight,' says Puck.

'They won't know that,' states Robert emphatically. 'Please, just give us a go.'

'You know the risk,' says Hunter, standing. 'So be it,' and he reaches over to shake Robert and Shauna's hands.

We held the challenges that afternoon. I didn't win the run, but I came second to Seamus the Red which is pretty good considering.

Hunter chose not to compete which only means that no one else gets a go at his title until next year. I did bloody badly at the staff – distracted I suppose.

Sheila won the filíocht challenge *again*. I don't believe it.

Rowan and Puck and Gypsy and the other six Lost people took the brew as the sun set, and made it through to begin a life of a long, long time.

Jack refused, saying maybe next time to Brighid, who finally came back from wherever in the draíocht that she'd gone since the meeting. I figure she knows the pattern, she's got that look in her eyes.

I passed on the message to Annis who just smiled.

Robert and Shauna died from the brew. Died quietly journeying the Otherworld, smiles on their faces as they traveled beyond our reach.

The end of a line of great kings. The end of the Guardians.

Everybody gathered on the third day, when we put them into the earth, to bid them fair skies and a strong wind at their backs on the journey into the West.

No one's certain about the future.

Hunter never said a word to anyone else about what he'd told me.

On the bus, back on the highway it's pretty late so there's no traffic. Jack's at the wheel with Matt playing the low whistle softly in the seat beside him.

I'm trying to get to sleep like most of the rest of our company. Brighid and Hunter are the only ones down back here to be still sitting up. They haven't talked for days.

'I know it all,' I overhear Brighid say quietly to the big man.

'So,' he replies quietly.

'Hmm,' she sighs.

I know where this is going. I know it all too well.

7

FOREST PEOPLE

LORE

CRACK. THE RESIN BURIED DEEP within the log could no longer remain dormant under the intensity of the fire. The tiny explosion adjusted the blaze in the hearth. The embers momentarily opened their impossibly red eyes and a shower of sparks sprayed up the chimney.

Fáith is not distracted. Not one part of her. She holds the ash shaft securely in the vice while she shaves the fluff from within the follicle of the feather.

She takes it gently between the tweezers and releases the vice. She uses the tiny badger hair brush to line the follicle with a breath of glue. She fixes it to the wood, equidistant from the two white gander feathers. They face towards the bow. The black, the king fletch—the goose fletch—faces away. She does this arrow after arrow. Hour after Hour.

Outside the cottage is a world of silence. That certain blue that only seen on a frozen landscape at night. No wind. Utter stillness. The air thin. Birch and rowan bejeweled with icicles, spruce tufted with snow, the ground thick with it, both powder and firn.

The wolf lies on his rug at the grate, his lids half closed, his head on his forepaws. Both he and Fáith seem at peace, relaxed. Like sister and brother from the same mother their hearing is flawless. If there is a sound to be heard—the jangle of a bridle, the kick of a heel against a flank, the sound of breath they will hear that. From miles away. Whether on foot, on horseback or riding the reindeer-pulled sled, if the otherkind try to approach the two will be gone. There is no other way to travel this far into the forest. Any petrol-driven vehicle will run out of fuel at least a day before it reached this remoteness.

Fáith was not born here but she has grown up here. She is this place.

Her Da had lived to his fortieth year, but her mam had died when her daughter was just one year old.

Her Da and his wolves had stalked the kill with Fáith secured to his back in a finely crafted leather-and-weave cradle board. To get her used to their territory. Her mam had hunted those razor-toothed, iron traps the otherkind had ordered set to catch the wolves. Or the people.

She'd missed the one that took her leg off at the ankle. She died before Fáith's Da found her, the blood like crimson butterflies on the snow, her mam seemingly the creature itself, just sleeping.

Fáith knew they were after her. The Church. That crazy species of two-legged otherkind with their vengeful deity. Their belief that their species was superior and chosen. That hers must be saved. Brought in and saved. She knew they lied about her people, *anLucht Súille*. Indigenous hunter-gatherers.

Wolves are always wild. There is no such thing as a tame wolf. When the otherkind had first contact with *anLucht Súille* they had thought the wolves that traveled with them were domesticated. They shot anyway and those not struck down had fled, the people not shot rounded up and herded. They had been forced to walk that long walk. It was only then that the otherkind realized that two-legged and four were pack and that both were wild. It was the word *wild* that was the confusion. Tame was what? Safe?

Tame is not safe, Fáith muses as she attaches a nock and a broadhead to each of the twenty-four arrows. *Tame is vulnerable*.

To make this forest safe for their enterprise the Patron, the title of the leaders of those who claimed *anLucht Súille's* ancestral lands—before the burning of vast tracts of forest, before the railway, before the cities—had devised the systematic hunting of her people. When they worked out how to parley, the interpreters gave *anLucht Súille* two choices: adapt and settle in the cities or live on the land allotted them. Land without forest called a reservation. They were to make do and not hunt anymore. They were to have nothing to do with wolves.

Some of her people thought adaptation might provide better for their families, in the fast-growing cities. Working for the foreigners. They left the reservation. They lived in small rooms, crowded, in upright coffins. Cinderblock flats. Alcoholic. Chrome. Suicide. Shunned because of the slight slant of their eyes, the clan tattoos.

Thought of as barbarians. Eaters of the raw dead.

They ate what the shop owners sold them. They ran up debts because they did not understand money. White flour and bread. Sugar, a new food. Canned staples. What meat they could pilfer was old or rancid. No fish. They worked the roads to pay their bills. They had nothing. A relentless cycle. They were subject to disease, to liver failure and diabetes. They got fat and died young. Their children lost their language and their lore.

Many of the people who used to live where Fáith now sleeps had fought back. They had fought from the tree line, not wanting to venture onto the wrongness that was now pasture where once the forest had dwelled, habitat and mother, from before time. They all died. They brought down a merciless punishment on the women and children, the elders, who had not fought also. It was all slaughter then. Just forty-seven years ago. The otherkind had guns, Fáith's people the axe and the bow.

Fáith's parents were second generation reservation people. They had become lovers because their own parents were all close: knowledge holders. From different clans they shared secrets freely now. Those secrets, and *anLucht Súille* lore of both clans, were told to Fáith's mam and Da. In case of hope. In case of a future. So that the knowledge of who the people truly were did not vanish from the world.

Her parents had escaped, and it was years before their absence came to the attention of the authorities. Punishment had been the murder of all the known knowledge holders, including Fáith's grandparents.

Her mam and Da had known how to call to the wolf in the

correct manner. Politely. How to honor the hunt trails. To honor the kill. To stay alive. To live well. To follow the dragon lines, the ancient ley lines the nomadic must travel to honor the seasons of the year.

The wolves understood the nuance of the language of their two-legged cousins. They had hunted and shared the hearth with them for millennia. They remembered. They led the runaways to the furthest, still untainted territory within the forest where they lived in isolation. Where Fáith was born. The wolf, upon his rug, is the son of the pup placed within her crib on the day of her birth. Fáith has lived twenty winters and this pup, five.

The second-last thing she does for the night is to clean the tools her Da had made for her. Put them into their individual compartments of the chamois bag with the straps. Stow this into the pack—tough leather, reindeer hide—that she keeps beside the door alongside the quiver of twenty-four arrows, just below the frame that supports the recurve bow. Her Da had made that for her from the wood of the mountain ash just a year ago. He had crafted it especially for her. She was given it the night of her initiation. The night her Da had inked the first of her clan tattoos into the skin of her face with the ink made from the soot of the mountain ash. The perfect blue line from her left ear, across her cheek, over her nose just below her eyes and on to her right ear.

Just months after he did this for her he died. She gave him to the crows and hawks and bears, the way she had been taught, for all of us are food.

The last thing she does is to pull down her snowshoes. The wolf is instantly on his feet. He prances to the door in anticipation.

They move in silence deeper into the forest. Far enough so that the smell of their urine will not attract anything back to the cottage.

That night they sleep curled together on the rug before the hearth, like puppies, the smoldering back log sending off no sparks. This is how it is done.

The next day they hunt from the hint of silver-pale predawn until well into the blue and shadow of the night. Fáith carries all her weapons and wears her pack on her back. Game is scarce this deep into winter. All they bring down are two hares. White. Only visible by their movement. Fáith shoots the one and has time to slit it from throat to groin, gut it and skin it before the wolf finally stops tormenting the other, with a defining snap to its neck. A race the hare would have won a month earlier or a month later.

The wolf carries his quarry back, tossing it high in the air and pretending it is still alive. Fáith eats the rich, warm liver and heart of her kill, tossing the remaining offal to the wolf. She guts and skins his trophy before returning it to him whole. As is fair.

Winter fur. Good hides. She will use them to thicken the lining of her boots.

Splitting the silence of the night, the jangle of harness. A baying. Fáith and the wolf are instant stillness. Which direction? They waited. To the south was the high squeal of a winter hawk echoes through the rarefied air. A warning.

Now attuned, the pair wait. Their enemies are many miles away.

Still unknowing. The advantage is with the hunted.

The whuffle of a horse's nostrils, the snow giving way beneath hooves. Four horses. Two hounds. That means four men; less probably because they'll need at least one horse for supplies. Even odds if confronted. Unless they have rifles. They are bound to have rifles.

And the scent of blood is upon the snow. The red of it a deep stain. None of the hunters will know what had been killed or by what. Woman and the wolf still hold the upper hand.

The otherkind will burn the cottage but she is not attached.

They run. Most of the night. Mile after mile deeper into the snow, higher into the alpine raw.

Daylight is four hours of grey becoming white becoming grey with no horizon within the perpetual mountain. What's the plan? None. Not anymore. They follow the caribou trails north through nights lit by green and amber borealis, grandmother of rivers, teaching the deepest ones the sorcery of silence that the brooks and burns are too young to comprehend. It is the silence of the oldest boulders that pock this tundra.

She gathers kindling and easy to snap elder wood, uptorn roots from this or that ancient storm for nightlong warmth. She builds their fire to the side of the entrance of shelter to dissuade the curious predator from trespassing a sleep of peace. These sanctuaries are lava tubes, remnants of the mountain's savage and molten history, countless millions of years ago.

Freedom. No domination. She will not let them down. If they are all that remains, so be it. They are these mountains, this snow, the ways of the thunder and the black water beneath the frozen river. The two are bonded for life and, while with this land there is no death.

They sleep curled together for warmth beneath a vault of the ochre handprints of once-upon-a-time children.

They are watched, from the tree line, by a woman, her face tattooed in lines and dots and totem animals. With her are two wolves. They'll wait patiently, until their cousins awake, to take them home.

8

WHAT WOULD HAPPEN IF EVERYBODY STARTED TELLING THE TRUTH?

TRAINING

INTRODUCTION

IF YOU DON'T WATCH MOVIES THAT reveal a future dark and dangerous, controlled and grey, with black-masked cops wielding lasers and stun guns, that doesn't mean that millions of others avoid that film. Are entertained. Some worry. A few realize how close we are to that virtual future. One could almost become paralyzed. Paranoid. Convinced, because virtual means almost, and I am old enough to remember that eventualities occur because of somebody's capacity to speculate. You see I was born into a world with hardly any plastic, no TV. No mobile phones, no computers. Can you imagine?

So, peer a little deeper into the future and ask yourself if you've done enough. Imagine, if you can, the seventh generation. Does it matter that your name is not remembered? No. But I'm aware that one person (just one person) can affect an incalculable number of people with the right keys. The very thing that affects our species the most, outside of the necessities of food, sex, shelter, sleep and health, is excitation. And what excites? Interaction. Doesn't matter with what. And what is the key here? Communication. Whether through words, gesture, expression, sensation or manipulation, communication is our species' most exciting (and devastating) tool.

PART 1

BABBLE

There's too much talking. And talking, much of the time, has taken on a seriously flawed agenda. Either personal or social propaganda in an era of sensory assault. I would be naïve to believe that people had not used lying or distortions of the truth for gain or profit (in whatever form) for a very long time. One merely needs to know sufficiently of history to get the big picture. But... At no other known time has there been an atmosphere so degraded, so filled with energetic chatter, so burdened with radio-waves, microwaves, electrical interference as now. Not that I know of, that is.

THE BIGGER PICTURE

Time and space and matter are all made up of energy in some great dance and song. Light joins the festival telling us, as a species of life, just how fine is starlight. Everything that *is* emits. Everything in the continuum of living and dying (which is all progression from something to something else) is entwined with everything else in an endless season of energetic symbiosis, constantly changing in patterns that the naked eye cannot see but that our bodies know. Our DNA hold the knowledge of forever (Big Bang being merely a theory of possible beginnings because what comes from nothing).

As an animist I also understand that nothing is inanimate. Everything has soul. Physical forms might not all breathe the way that we do but in a universe so complex, who would have the audacity as to assume we were special anyway? Suns and stars and tables and worms, mold and plastic and cold, cold iron – all emit. All express energy in whatever their state of growth or entropy. One photon a trillion light years away from Alpha Centauri dances a pattern. Another photon another trillion light years away knows about this because all expressions of energy nestle in a sea of infinite space that is very good at not losing anything.

LOCALIZING

Earth (Anima Mundi) is life. If it isn't here we don't know about it. We are getting to the point that we think we understands an awful lot about energy, from particle physics and quantum mechanics to chaos theory. And more often the new sciences recognize that energy and our understanding of consciousness are not separate. That nothing is separate, but inter-relative, therefore our symbiosis with Earth is, of course, mutual.

Our relationship with Earth is as seriously damaged as a pair of friends where one person does all the talking and the other ends up very bored because they are being treated like a wall. Lovers playing power-over games. Politicians pretending to listen to the people they are meant to represent but who go ahead and make war anyway. Scientists devoutly inventing another noxious toxin and telling us how beneficial it will all be. And hardly anyone is listening to other voices because, should they, the ramifications to greed and avarice would be staggering.

PERSONALIZING

The following is all practical work

CHECK YOUR CURRENT REALITY:
QUESTIONS TO ASK

1 Who do you live with and what is your relationship to these people? Is your relationship to those with whom you live different to the relationship you have with your friends? If so, how and why? Do you hold a job? If so who are you around your workmates and employers? If you are studying what is your relationship to a. the tutors and b. the subject matter of your study? Is the subject matter of your study aligned with a vocation?

2 What is the quality of communication like with those in question one? Is the quality based on a pecking order of imposed household authority? What are your responses when faced with dispute? Is it debate, argument, someone walking out and slamming the door, one of

you waiting to see who says sorry first, resentment, guilt, anxiety, violence, boredom? Is your household comfortable with silences or do others think there's a problem if one of you is not speaking for their own reasons? Do any of you seek to interfere with another's choices without discussion?

What is the color of your conversations with your friends? Do you ever branch into dangerous topics that could offend another's viewpoint? Do you regularly discover things to talk about? Are you comfortable with these people when there's nothing to say?

Is your employment satisfying? Why? Do you question the motives of the business? How do you relate to authority; your own or that of others?

Do you ever really listen to your seemingly-random thoughts? If so, can you discern the different *layers* of thought?

Do you think about what you say when you say it, or do you find yourself repeating material in a repertoire?

Do you ever communicate, internally, with someone or something that you know is not you?

What, to you, constitutes authority?

Do you have unique thoughts and/or *original* conversations or are they based on pre-learned parameters?

Do you question everything that you are told or taught?

Do you question yourself on issues, ideals, ideologies, beliefs, ethics, moralities and information upon which you base your judgments or opinions? Do you change when the above is undermined, or do you insist on being seen as consistent?

When listening to another person speaking, do you listen without bias?

Answering these questions can change you. Especially if you allow yourself to answer freely and to enter debate regarding the questions, your answers and what you really feel in the depths of yourself. Do you even care? Does it matter? Does anyone you know care? Are you living in a vacuum?

THE PRACTICE

The practice has nothing to do with talking and everything to do with listening – listening very deeply.

Listening deeply requires that you use more than your ears. Listening requires that you use your hearing in conjunction with your eyes, your sense of atmosphere, your gut.

THE PRACTICE REQUESTS THAT...

First, you initiate no conversations, you only respond to what is said to you, you do not automatically think of what you will say next, you recognize your pre-conditioned biases and emotional responses you respond to all conversations without pre-conceived parameters of relationship.

Second, you observe the body language of the person with whom you are engaged in conversation, you remain aware of the spaces between your bodies as this is a strong indicator of the emotional state of the person towards you, you remain aware of your bodily responses to the conversation and learn to trust them – they are a truer receptivity barometer than your intellect when any emotional content enters into the conversation, you never pre-judge a person by the glamor they present, rather you remain alert to the equality of all people, no matter how educated in the so-called western modality.

EXAMPLES OF ROLE

The Arguer: debate, keeping the object of debate at the constant foreground of conversation, does not lead to argument unless the participants become emotionally attached to being right. It is no longer, then, a debate but a debacle that will leave both or all parties debilitated.

The Manipulator: emotional manipulation utilizes many criteria: guilt, flattery, conspiracy, destructive criticism, arrogance, vulnerability, constant agreement, denial, comparison – you can tell which is which, by the inflation/deflation ratio.

The Quoter: this person will use 'the big guns' of authority by quoting the works of others as a reference upon which to base their opinions.

The White-Lighter: well, mostly they don't engage, they just tell you what's good for you and talk at you about stuff that makes them feel good about themselves.

The Perennial Parent: is constantly thinking they know what's best for others, based on their own experience, socially, spiritually, morally and emotionally. This behavior seeks to impose uniformity onto individuality without recourse to differences. Many politicians and religious leaders do this. As do people with something to gain. As do those who need a mirror to their own psyches.

The Victim: there are two kinds of victim in the world. Those with choices and those without. Those people who have choices can choose to change their current realities, but the Victim will not, preferring to use that behavior to attract sympathy, to control another.

Real victims (of any species or life-form) have no choices. They are legion, and altering the ways we both communicate, and listen, are two of their chances of escape. They do not have a voice. They are not heard.

What you will be doing by actively engaging in this experiment, is to break down, or through, conditioning. You will be altering your emission – your harmonic – and that will influence the collective field. Enough alteration: overall change to the human harmonic affecting life.

SCIENCE AND MYSTICISM

Each person is born with a talent, and once that talent is realized and expressed one's life takes on meaning. No one person's talent is more important than another's, they are simply different, and those differences are what make people exciting.

Sometimes a talent can seem like a gift and other times it feels like a curse. It feels like a curse when one is unable or incapable of following through on realizations. For example, I can predict the future for others, but I cannot prevent what seems like misfortune from happening. I can hear the desolation emitting from the gorillas in a zoo, but I cannot release them. I can pick up the despair of the refugees in enforced detention centers, but my only recourse is protest.

I hear them in the voices of nature. I listen to animals and we talk the same language of feeling and sensation, necessity and humour. It's people who are in a serious state of communication-crisis. So often, what is said is not what is meant, or is said for the sake of talking, or is what I call the broken record conversation, or what is said has a hidden agenda of want. Conversations with people who have been damaged, emotionally, and who have never released their attachment to the experience that caused the dysfunction can be deeply akin to psychic vampires. What all of them have in common – what everyone has in common – is that they emit. These emissions are what are currently distorting life's patterns, and this will affect the future; this *is* affecting the future.

WHAT SOUND IS

In 1787, the jurist, musician and physicist Ernst Chladni published *Entdeckungen über die Theorie des Klanges* or (Discoveries Concerning the Theory of Music). In this and other pioneering works, Chladni laid the foundations for that discipline within physics known now as acoustics, the science of sound. Among Chladni's successes was the discovery of a way to make sound visible. With the help of a violin bow, which he drew perpendicularly across the edge of flat plates covered with sand, he produced those patterns and shapes which today are called *Chladni Figures*. What was the significance of this discovery? Chladni demonstrated once and for all that sound does affect physical matter and that it has the quality of creating geometric patterns.

This is called *cymatics* (<Gk *Kyma* or *ta kymatika*: matters pertaining to waves). The study of wave phenomena is a science that was pioneered by Hans Jenny (1904-1972), a Swiss medical doctor and natural scientist. He conducted experiments animating inert powders, pastes, and liquids into life-like, flowing forms, which mirrored patterns found throughout nature, art and architecture. What's more, these patterns were created using simple sine wave vibrations within the audible range. What you see is a physical representation of vibration, or how sound manifests into form through the medium of various materials.

Dr. Jenny's methodology was meticulous, well documented, and totally repeatable. His fascinating body of work offers profound insights into both the physical sciences and esoteric philosophies. It illustrates the very principles which inspired the ancient Greek philosophers Heraclites, Pythagoras and Plato, on down to Giordano Bruno and Johannes Kepler, the fathers of modern astronomy.

EMISSION

The easiest and most familiar way to study vibration is through sound. Just as the many and varied alphabets of the world encompass all possible words in verbal language, the octave structure encompasses all possible vibrations of sound, and reveals the simple way that they fit together. Chaos theory might call the octave an *attractor*, meaning that all vibrations of sound, however chaotic or random they might be from one to the next, must be *attracted* into the octave structure.

An identical level of this octave of vibration occurs in the visible light spectrum, where we recognize seven colors before encountering other, more subtle levels (or octave of vibrations) such as infrared, ultraviolet, X-rays, gamma waves. Science tells us that packets or units of energy known as *photons* form the basis for light, and we now know that the *frequency* of the photons that create visible light are simply a *finer octave of vibration* than the sound frequencies of the musical octave. In other words, you could take the numerical ratios between each note in the musical Diatonic scale and double them many times over, and eventually you would find the same, identical ratios between the vibrational speeds of the light spectrum. The only difference is the magnitude- sound is vibrating much more slowly, whereas light is vibrating much more quickly.

THE SOUND OF MAGIC

Clairaudience, clairvoyance, clairsentience: the same but different.

Philosophy is written in this grand book – I mean universe – which stands continuously open to our gaze, but which cannot be understood unless one first learns to comprehend the language in which it is written. It is written in the language of mathematics, and its characters are triangles, circles and other geometric figures, without which it is humanly impossible to understand a single word of it; without these, one is wandering about in a dark labyrinth. Galileo (1623).

If, sitting here, I was to prophesy about the next fifty years only, I could do so with a probability ratio, oh randomly, of about a 99.9% certainty, we're in for big trouble. It doesn't take a genius to figure out that right now, in the early years of the 21st Century, we're at a point of environmental and social critical mass. I could throw up my arms and get really upset about all the issues facing life (*all* life) but that would only add to the problem and, it wouldn't make sense. I have read tarot for other people for decades. They come from everywhere, all walks of life, hold a myriad of differing viewpoints on life, the universe and everything, and year after year that which is foretold comes to pass. How? What is it that allows a seemingly random shuffle of seventy-eight cards to predict events that seemingly have not yet happened?

The events have already happened.

MATTER AND ENERGY

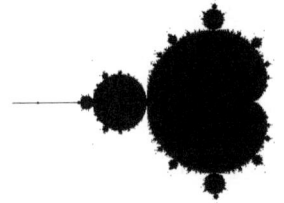

I listened to a couple of scientists being interviewed on ABC Radio National back in the 1980's. They were traveling Australia on a discussion tour. They had done studies of differing forms of divination for a year and had concluded that "tarot defies the law of probability" more than any other form of foretelling. Up until then I'd always wondered, but had never had the keys, to look for answers to the mystery of what I do. I undertook some basic study of quantum physics and read Gleick's book on *Chaos Theory*, pondered, in awe, such things as the Mandelbrot Set and Fractal Geometry.

If we consider the theory of the *Big Bang*, then light (remembering that it's a vast thing and the naked eye sees only a very small section), which is both particle and wave, occurred instantaneously throughout the universe. Matter, on the other hand, seems to be taking its time catching up, which is why our universe is said to be in a continuous state of expansion.

As nothing comes from nothing we were the *Big Bang*, albeit in a different state of vibration: both light and matter on an arrow-flight through conceptual evolution, however virtual. Now whether we consider our current selves as human or otherwise is irrelevant; whatever we even *contemplate* our ancestors as having been is irrelevant. What *is* most profound is our having been there, because if we hadn't been there we wouldn't be here now. The mere fact that our hemoglobin contains iron; that our insides slosh around in vast quantities of a fusion of hydrogen[2] and oxygen (and that hydrogen is what fuels stars) is fact. That our bodies follow a seemingly adequate set of parameters and reproduction indicates that they remember having been around forever… and that surely after several billion we've experienced most everything in one manner or another.

When a person shuffles my tarot cards, they are sorting them into an order. Because everything has been experienced that person doesn't need to look at the images, like a very proficient pianist does not have to look at where their fingers are going (and in some cases to look would be to stop the music) because the music is *in* them. I interpret what the person is telling me because quite often when you're involved in your life you lack objectivity. This is where the strange part comes in. And I've wondered about this all my life: is it a case of the chicken or the egg?

COLLAPSING THE WAVE: THOUGHT TO SPEECH
With a Pinch of Spell casting

Have you ever heard it said that to name the thing is to empower the thing? That to speak it will either prevent a thing from happening, or else, if you speak a thing, you will cause it to happen (hence *touch wood*)?

Not only is it the basis for spell casting it is also founded on an interesting theory put forward by Dr. Darryl Reanney in his book *The Music of the Mind*: that thought is like light and travels at the same speed and that speaking collapses the wave giving it a semblance of matter. Once spoken, never unspoken. Once spoken, the thought becomes interwoven with the fabric of our atmosphere as a frequency (please see Part 1 as a reference to babble) and can interfere with material reality.

Consequently, once I say aloud what I see or experience in tarot it enters time. Still as an energy (like light) that the individual will walk into sooner or later, it will be recognized as it happens. Therefore retrospectively, as the present moment is already the past it has already happened once spoken.

It's the same with causing events to occur by way of the use of verbal magic. One can enter a spell into an average conversation and probably no one else will ever know. It all depends on what is said and how it is said but the reality is that I *know* I'm creating a loop: NOW→THEN→NOW. It all depends on how we understand progression. When we *really* throw away the illusion of linear time all things are valid, it's merely a matter of when.

To achieve a conscious transition from the fate of linear time one simply needs to look at life, the seasons, the natural configuration of existence: it either spirals, cycles or unfolds. When and why did the line become such a god?

THOUGHT INTO MATTER

Propaganda is one of the more potent influencers of contemporary western culture. Media and the advertising industries are the current dispensers of doctrines of acceptability. Throughout the centuries people have been told what they should or should not do and are threatened with the inventions of damnation, starvation or torture for bucking the rules. These inventions are projections of consciousness. I know this could sound trite, but it is people who make tables, and tables began in the minds of their inventors. Therefore, to think a thing is to trigger an act of creation when the thought is manifest into a material reality.

The future is the product of all that precedes it – it is a concept. It is therefore very important that we participate in the art of creating events yet to come into existence through our current actions and awareness. This requires conscious choices in every situation, no matterwhat our lot in life. It requires conscious responses to sensory input, specifically, in relation to words, realizing that Logos is as easily manipulated as a puppet.

PART 2

DESPAIR

Practical healing

When, either personally or collectively, the illusion of either abandonment or disconnection (sometimes both) mental illness manifests and expresses itself in a tapestry of dysfunction. This disease is despair and a necessary step in the eradication of despair, is to first recognize that it is present, either in yourself, your family, your peers, your community, the current zeitgeist or the demands of a society. To do this you monitor your attitude and outlook on everything for a set number of weeks/months. You will, of course, be affected by news and advertising, which often depict the world (in the former) in a disadvantaged state and (in the latter) what you will need to own or to look like to be on the winning side. There is no point blinkering oneself throughout this training. It is also important to keep eyes wide, wide open; to learn as much as one can about the soul-illness afflicting our mutual species. It seems to present itself in several ways.

Apathy. Constant assault from myriad media sources can trigger a form of apathy whereby people can watch horrific scenes of barbarity and brutality that eventually, seemingly bounce off the psyche... but do they? How can they? What really happens is more insidious: acceptance that these behaviors are validated by their continuum. The training you undertake in ridding yourself of despair is all about seeing clearly what is happening but realizing that you are not a participant in the process.

Accumulation (or, when is enough, enough?) The propaganda of advertising is not about *you* benefiting from a product, remember that, rather it is about a chain of profit that has its own best interest at heart. That chain of profit includes people who produce *nothing* but who benefit enormously from those who do. And by creating fear. Finding a level of contentment with your possessions and consciously understanding that you need no more is a powerful thing. It allows *you* the security of simplicity and it means you no longer feed the beast. To purchase your goods directly from the grower or the manufacturer means that you are respecting their work, feeding their families and denying improper investment used for such things as war, environmental rape, the lining of the pockets of the greedy and any of an incalculably vast arsenal of destructive research and development (including the still-prevalent use of vivisection).

Debt. Have you heard of the term *usury*? I realize that it is considered as the 'illegal' charging of excessive interest on loans but who is it that decides what is excessive? Is *'a profit of $2.192 billion…'* in one year excessive? Is: "The Reserve Bank found the big four banks enjoy an implicit government subsidy worth up to $4 billion dollars a year," said Mr Oquist. This amount of money is SPARE MONEY. It will be used for investment. Do you know where this money will be invested? Do you know how this profit was accrued?

Every time you take out a loan, or purchase using credit, you are indebting, even enslaving, yourself to others. In the current climate of company CEO's claiming bonuses in the millions of dollars you might want to ask yourself: *How do I fare?* When will be your next holiday? What is your quality of life like? I'm not necessarily talking about issues of which you are unaware but, so far, have I managed to get you thinking?

Please note that some of the following topics will overlap each other.

Relationships. Communicate without fear. Communicate without the need to manipulate. Respect silence when there is nothing to say. Whether we are talking about an intimate relationship, the relationship between family, between friends, between associates – the way to understand relationships, and not lose yourself somewhere in these relationships, is to know three things:

1. There is *always* going to be a pecking order within any relationship. This is not a power, or a power-over, phenomenon but a biological one. It cannot be controlled, and neither can the conflict that can, and invariably will, arise because of it. Therefore, understanding it is your first line of least resistance. No relationship is permanent, and no relationship will remain fixed to any idea any of us may consider. False relationships are those based on power over others.

2. Every species has a pecking order. The problem for people is that *we* are animals, and generally we don't remember that. We have been conditioned, through both the entertainment industry and religions, of the idealization of love. Many in intimate relationships find themselves in the dominant/submissive role. This always leads to conflict. When sexually active people mark each other with their scents (in effect: marking their territory) and someone else enters the picture there will be conflict unless the couple band together, like a wolf-pair, to attain a specific outcome (scenario irrelevant). In the case of a couple without children there is likely to be little conflict unless outsiders attempt to lay a scent. In the case of a couple *with* children? Well, here's the reason for a couple of millennia of discord or oppression.

3. In most other animal species, the breeding female is the dominant member of the pack, herd, barnyard and the males will always fight for her favors, therefore establishing their own pecking order. This is not our history. The male of our species has been placed in an unnatural state of dominance. Currently the western world is undergoing a crisis of sexuality (specifically in heterosexual society) because, again taking animal behavior into account, no species, other than humans, have sex with one animal or the other lying on their back. The flipping of an animal onto its back is a threat. In another powerful turn, same-sex relationships and gender variations alter the perspective of what, even fifty years ago, would have been predictable in sexual relationships.

SUGGESTED SOLUTIONS

Share your living-space with several people, setting clear boundaries of mutual responsibility and gain. If assisting good friends or family to move into a new dwelling be certain to lay your scent on the dwelling by either cleaning, helping to place objects and furniture, cooking a meal for them using their appliances. This will ascertain you both feel, and are, welcome whenever you return. Respect for each other's needs for independence and spontaneity, do not lean or rely on each other, rather be together for the sake of simply that.

Recognize the pecking order that is *natural* between you, and your near associates, but do not allow it to manipulate or over-ride the uniqueness of everyone involved. Communicate freely (and that does not imply talking a lot) but do not invade another's need for solitude or silence when that need is obvious.

IMPERMANENCE

Many relationships *do* have a life-span and attempting to hold onto them when they cease to be relevant to either/any party involved is kind of like not burying or performing an appropriate death-rite with a corpse: sooner or later the thing will become repugnant. Quite often the severance process at the completion of a relationship is painful. So be it. Mourning is a natural way of dealing with letting go. Respect of both the self, and the process of change, is how one transforms through change.

There is an astrological cycle called the *Mars Cycle* which is approximately two and a quarter, solar years. Two opposing phenomena occur: This is when most relationships that are unsuccessful are supposed to end. That's when you will feel it. If a breeding female, whose biology is switched on to conception, has not been inseminated during that time she is likely to seek out a more desirable mate. If she is not trapped in cultural expectations. When an individual or group relocate, and they remain in the new location for the *Mars Cycle*, they will have bonded with the environment and will experience deep distress if forced to move on.

FALSE RELATIONSHIPS

We encounter these at all levels of society – governments, business, family, institutional religion, within many education systems, socially. These superficial hierarchies are established for the purposes of control or greed (perhaps both). In an ideal world there *is* a need for leadership, but that leadership ought to be based on the transparency, wisdom and proven adroitness of an individual. On their *consistency*. In an ideal society those leaders are not better than anyone else but are clear on the responsibilities based on integrity. Leaders are good leaders when they don't *need* to lead, and they realize that they are merely good at what they do and are reliable within the expertise of that leadership.

Parents quite often demand that their children conform to authority that is not gained through example but through force (sometimes physical, usually psychological), as do many institutionalized educators, as do politicians and employers.

Observation, on your part, of the behavior and body-language of others will allow you to understand any situation and to either extricate yourself from it or mold your behavior (not necessarily your true self) to fit the circumstances.

DEATH

Despair often walks with the person who has been taught to fear death. Through consciously accepting the organic nature of death (and that everything does it, therefore it is natural), and deciding to live your life gloriously, death can be known for what it is – a breaking down of organic matter into that which it is forever becoming something else.

Religions and New Age movements place an inordinate focus on retaining one's individuality (as it is understood) after body-death and there are, therefore, a plethora of ideologies and theories concerning an *After-Life*. I ask you to contemplate: when is there no life? What constitutes no life? When is there *not* life? Is it necessary to *believe* in an *After-Life* as distinct from life? Do we know all there is to know? There is nothing 'after' life because life is perpetual; eternal. And, besides, it's not like body-death is something anyone really ought to worry about because it's going to happen sooner or later. In the meantime, what about the *quality* of living?

A LACK OF BODY-KNOWLEDGE

When your health or well-being is taken out of our hands; when we do not know sufficiently about our own bodies to ascertain their functions; when we accept, blindly, the authority of others over our own, we allow the demon of despair to have itself a party.

Change the situation.

I was once told by a doctor to whom I was teaching fitness, that throughout the entirety of his medicinal training he only spent around forty hours learning about nutrition. Death is an integral facet of good health. Without sufficient decaying matter—compost—the earth's ability to sustain and grow food is diminished, as are the food's nutritional elements when they are consumed. Growing food is an unsurpassed act of creativity and anarchy. It's witchcraft at its deepest, and as Frank Herbert said in his unpublished notes: *A requirement of creativity is that it contributes to change. Creativity keeps the creator alive.*

MULENGRO

The spelling mulengro is a shortening of the form mulengero. This shortened form is used quite commonly in some varieties of Romani < mulhengero mulo (fog ghost) <Mulengero Di (All Souls Day) < mulo (dead) [these terminologies are from the Burganland Romani dialect]

Mulengro is like a disease passed from one person to another using seven dysfunctional manipulations:

>   ENVY
>   GREED
>   GUILT
>   DECEIT
>   DENIAL

EXPECTATION
ASSUMPTION

When someone attempts to entice, control, coerce or otherwise warp seeming-facts to suit an agenda they will use one or more of these techniques. The only way to prevent despair from overwhelming our well-being is to cease Mulengro in our lives. I've done it; several of my students have done it; most of my friends have stopped it.

The outcome to being infected by Mulengro is *always* resentment, rejection, blame and, despair. And Mulengro *is* infectious.

Mulengro is like the *Karpman Drama Triangle*:

I read an article about a couple living together. I'll call them Gabe and Kelly to ensure gender neutrality because this happens in every partnership at least once.

Kelly is at home and Gabe phones from the office, explaining there is an after-work function they were required to attend, and it could go until late.

Kelly asks, So Gabe, will you be home for dinner?

I doubt is, says Gabe, so don't bother cooking for me unless you want to. I can always microwave it later.

Okay, says Kelly.

The problem begins when Kelly thinks to make dinner for two anyway, just in case Gabe comes home unexpectedly and is hungry. Partners do that for each other, right? They love each other.

But Gabe does not come home and does not call.

Kelly, alone, does not get on with the evening and read a book. The thought is there, but thoughts also stray to the time, and how late Gabe is. And has there been an accident? Or is Gabe having an affair? Or…

Finally, exhausted, Kelly goes to bed but cannot sleep because Gabe's absence is now a monster.

At 3 a.m. Gabe comes home drunk, closes the door quietly, removes the shoes and creeps upstairs to the bedroom. Kelly switches on the light.

Where were you? Why didn't you call me? I made us dinner anyway but then it just dried out and was ruined so I threw it away. Why are you so late? What have you been doing? I've been so worried. I didn't know whether to call the hospitals or your mother or what! I've been terrified you were mugged or dead.

I've got to pee, Gabe slurs, swaying towards the bathroom.

You're drunk! You've been partying and you're fucking drunk!

Kelly bursts into tears.

Gabe returns to the bedroom, undresses, gets into bed and is snoring in seconds.

What just happened? A happy couple is now on the slippery slide to an eventual end. Both are party to the drama triangle, also to every aspect of Mulengro. At one stage Kelly enacts all three characters of the triangle whilst both enact assumption, expectation denial and envy. Through Gabe's silence deceit is employed, as is denial and greed as Gabe *gaslighting* and *muting*.

GASLIGHTING

Named for a 1944 film called *Gas Light*. The term refers to a psychological abuse, and is used to describe an attempt to destroy another's perception of reality, very often by sociopaths or narcissists, but there are grades of that. Very often an individual will lie to another, thinking to save them from the hurt of knowing, for example, that they had sex outside the relationship and both do not want to admit it out of guilt, or wants to keep the external relationship as well as remain in the current partnership. The problem arises when one person's body (gut) gets the jitters. Adrenalin. Bodies read more than intellects and when one knows a partner as well as an intimate partner, or a parent/child relationship, bodies do the talking. Small things. A phone call not returned. A scent one cannot identify. Over time unknown patterns arise and the person being *gaslit* can become extremely ill. Anxiety. Fear. Confusion. If they ask the partner if something is going on they should know about and the partner says no. The relationship is, again, doomed. At the extreme, the victim of gaslighting kills themselves.

MUTING

When you have something important to discuss with a sibling, partner, offspring, parent, boss, misbehaving or inappropriate work colleague and they suggest you stop bitching, moaning, whining, complaining. They say, I don't want to discuss the matter, or you're talking out of turn, or I don't want to hear this again. Or, you want to keep your job? Do you do it?

It's aggression. It's avoidance. The person raising the topic is effectively shut down. It can be threatening. You run the risk of being cast out, unloved, unemployed, disbelieved. How do we function as a society?

The need to tell the truth. To also admit when we're wrong. To not inflict these psychological savageries onto people we love or admire when we would not inflict them on a total stranger.

Because all the above are dishonesties. They seek to avoid personal responsibility. Accountability.

AUTHORITY?

What connotations. The word *authority* has come to represent a pinnacle – the epitome of a powerful person. The word *authority* is very different, in truth, to a *master* (such as a master carpenter, a master of the sword, a master chef) because a person who has mastered a skill is a practitioner whereas, in many instances, an authority is someone with an opinion who confers with other people with opinions and who, therefore, could be considered educated in opinions. Of *course*, I'm generalizing but it is worth your consideration as quite often those who consider themselves authorities do not condone having that authority questioned and *that* is, and has been, despotism or tyranny or psychopathy. Whether the presumed authority is a parent, the president of a company or country, an educator, a five-star general, or a pope, it is the responsibility of a truthful person or society to consider the individual, or the institution, open to fallibility.

I once sat on the loo of a friend's house in Victoria pondering the poster he had on the back of the door. The image on the poster was of a skeleton in a bathtub in the bathroom of a hotel that is discovered in the far distant future by a team of archaeologists. They document the sarcophagus (the bathtub), the roll of paper used to send messages to the gods via an aqueduct (toilet paper and flush-toilet), mirror used for divination, various holy objects (like razor, toothbrush etc.) kept on the altar, the obvious sacredness of water (realized, of course, from the profusion of taps), the quirky plastic crown worn by the king or priest of this temple (the shower-cap). On and on went the description. I understood that no one could truly understand the past from the standpoint of the present and that all such sciences employ educated guesswork.

When I see a documentary on ancient people depicting them bent-over, ugly, hairy primates I tend to cringe as nothing in life is ungainly in its natural habitat so why depict humanity, alone, as having been so? And *primitive* is merely deemed as derogatory in comparison to us now. To take upon oneself the responsibility of informed questioning ensures that *authority* does not take upon itself the presumption it is better-than another, person, system, lore or knowledge just because it may not understand. It allows for possibilities, it allows for alternatives, it allows for error and it ensures that its own authority remains accountable.

RELIGION (from L: *religare*, to bind back)

THE JESUS MYTH

Pope Leo X, who reigned 1513-21, said: "It has served us well, this myth of Christ." By this he meant that over the centuries, the vatican managed to acquire enormous wealth and power in the name of a personality it called *Jesus Christ*. In the twentieth century, the man most responsible for making the Vatican a financial powerhouse was its investment manager, Bernardino Nogara. Speaking of him, one cardinal Spellman, of New York, once said, "Next to Jesus Christ, the best thing that ever happened to the catholic church is Bernardino Nogara." Anticipating that Europe was heading for war, Nogara invested heavily in armaments factories, buying several of them outright. This allowed the Vatican to reap huge profits when Mussolini invaded Abyssinia in 1935 and in World War II later.

RELIGIOUS FUNDAMENTALISM, DOGMA AND BIGOTRY

It is drummed into children in war-torn countries, brainwashing them into hating one another without them knowing exactly why. It is the arrogant racist who believes in an imperialist, white supremacy that presumes anything can be bought. It is in the neo-Nazi and the Ku Klux Klan. Fundamentalism is in the office worker next to you who feels her faith is superior to yours and that you will be damned for your viewpoint and your sexual activity and she, to a place thought of as paradise. Fundamentalism is the reason people mail anthrax to abortion clinics because they don't believe a woman should have a right to choose. Fundamentalism is the man who bullies, beats or represses his wife because he believes women are inferior – the source of all wickedness because of some Middle Eastern myth from life only knows how long ago – and passes on seeds of tyranny to his children. Fundamentalism is the people who mock same-sex love; people who shun unwed mothers, the poor, and those infected with HIV-AIDS calling such a terrible illness "the wrath of God". It is people who smile politely to those of another race in public but, condemn them in private purely because of the color of their skin or *their* religion. Religious fundamentalism; religious laws, rules, arrogance, moral condemnations.

 A very good way of controlling people, don't you think? Divide and rule? *Divide et impera*, the practice has been used socially, politically and militarily since documentation began. Philip II of Macedon (circa 365 BCE) is the first person quoted as utilizing the tactic. Divide us to conquer us. Diminish us. Instill doubt, envy, threat, fear. It is happening as I write, in politics. The year of this update is 2017 and politics wages a chess game of brinkmanship in league with big business and media. Do we buy into it? The challenge is to *not* allow it to. The challenge is to be very alert but to *not* become angry. They have us when that happens. Should we declare organic food our weapon, or peddle-power, or cloth bags instead of plastic, recycling over the next iPhone, if we should meet in an age of text-isolation, use pencils to remember how to write, gather in large numbers to protest the cruelty of factory farming and the imprisoning of refugees in offshore detention, if we could stand together so that education returns to being education instead of big business, not eat their garbage. Well, I'm with you on that. The same applies, I am stunned to be informed that, in the post twentieth century 'west', so-called spiritual practices known as paganism, shamanism, druidry, wicca and some groups that even call themselves witches, charge money to teach. To hold retreats. They sell products that we used to always make ourselves.

The challenge of this essay alone is for us to learn. For us to hold our freedom and not be undermined because we see what is being done. To learn and keep learning, Then, to unlearn when necessary; to deepen. To thunder into the future as creatures of art.

A future where wonder is revered, and the wildness and the beauty of life is honored, where such terms as *man conquers…*, *in the battle to control…* and *in the war against…* are no longer used to discuss natural phenomenon like mountains, space, death – actually, to not use this terminology for anything.

Religions? What *is* valid about them? Whom do they serve? Religions demand worship. They demand divisions and employ dualisms like good and evil, us and them, sacred or profane. Always divisive. Religion and the words *worship, faith, belief* all to go together. Inherent within these words is possibility of doubt. When we can gather for feasting and mutual learning, building a barn, a community, a cleaner environment, without religion to bind us, we'll have achieved a *grail quest*.

PART 3

THE POWER OF ONE

Do not think that because you are one person you cannot have a potent and intense effect on the future. My grandmother started me thinking about things mystical and magical when I was just eleven years old. She'd never taught her talent to anyone before me and she never taught anyone else after me. I've taught thousands of people throughout my life. Even more thousands, whom I've never met, have read the books I've written. I didn't start out thinking that was what was going to happen and ultimately it doesn't matter because I'm merely doing what I'm doing. Think of yourself as an atom. Small? Not really. Darryl Reanney, in *The Death of Forever* compared an atom's size thus: If you were to put a pin, head down in the ground in the middle of grand central stadium, the very tip of the pin would be the nucleus of an atom. The electrons are way outside the stadium moving so fast we only know they exist because of where they've been. Oppenheimer split it. The result, devastation. He is quoted as saying *Now I am become Death, the destroyer of worlds.* You will make a difference by living consciously and making clear, optimized choices, often by thinking about the next seven generations.

There is nothing without consequences and everything that we do have them. If none of us change the way we communicate between ourselves and our world then we're in an avalanche of trouble. I remember thinking, one time, on the eve of a rally on human rights, *So what? It doesn't matter if I don't attend, what's one person less?* Of course, it was just a fleeting thought. I knew I'd go, because if I didn't and nobody else did, there would be no hope.

One becomes two, two become ten, ten become ten thousand… And apartheid falls. Ten thousand become one million, and one million becomes humanity's next step to change.

CONCLUSION

SILENCE

Silence is, without doubt, the most important form of communication. In silence we can think. With silence we can dare to explore the thoughts deeply buried within the caves beneath the tundra that may hold answers like the truth in a situation of falsehood. Through silence we can also hear other things so vitally important like wind and rain and birdsong. Within silence is heard the voices of the spirits of place, the warnings of our ancestors and the stories, yet unsung.

Unless… If, as are in the lyrics of Simon and Garfunkle's song *The Sounds of Silence*, we understand that "silence, like a cancer grows", then it is the silence of opinion and opposition, out of fear of repercussion.

The differences between them are obvious, witches.

THE SONG OF LEVINGTON BLADE

Within the darkness one is waiting, a child of life unborn, alone,
till the season of confusion when the darkness turns to stone.
The one—the only covenant—that life called from the crown
will call you when it's ready, when its web is fully spun.
From the forest to the garden to the desert to the tomb,
to the place of revolution where no sun has ever shone.
Within the dance of death's embrace the seed is carried past the veil.
It is unfolding to its Pattern and a forest is its grail.

The song—not yet—of what will be, the child of life is forming
and you'll sing it with each other when it's born within its morning.

From the forest to the garden, to the desert to the sea,
to the place of resolution where the child will mother be
and another and another, in an endless symphony.
The seed is just one season to the seasons of the tree.
And the tree is of the forest of the earth that's yet to be.

Genesis | The Future, de Angeles, 2019)

9

AUTUMN EQUINOX

LORE

IT SEEMS A LONG TIME SINCE summer, so much has happened. I'd never thought that life could have gotten any more complicated than before I joined up with the Fianna. Still, it's done now.

Hunter says we'll be going back to the city before the winter and I guess I'm dreading it – no fond memories there. But that's the way of it. The band's gotta go where the work is and there's others lost besides me.

I love these people. Took me in without knowing anything about me. 'Least not anything I told them anyway.

Rowan found us this cottage and it's a good place. I'm always sensing the draíocht strongest in the autumn and the land here's alive with it.

I remember when we were driving up here and I commented on the thick fog that was making visibility on the road near impossible.

'Not fog,' Hunter had said softly from the driver's seat beside me.

'Is s-so,' I'd argued.

'Not fog,' yelled Rowan from down the back with the others. Annis had laughed and I'd sat brooding all scrunched up in my seat. She'd come up behind me and ruffled my hair and told me not to be so touchy.

The bus had labored at the steep climb and I remember wondering if it was going to make it all the way up the mountain to this mystery place that Rowan was so excited about. And I thought they'd been mucking me around about the fog till we drove right up through it.

Hunter stopped the bus at a roadhouse right in front of a tourist lookout, for coffee and a snack. We'd all clambered out into the hazy afternoon sunlight and I was struck by the crisp bite in the air; at how clean it was.

I wandered to the men's room down the side of the petrol outlet to relieve myself and splash water on my face, then I headed over to the lookout. Oh wow.

We were suspended on the brink of a sheer drop and we were up above the cloud. Great plumes, like towers, rose from the lazy white thickness below me. I leaned over the guardrail and got that weird sensation that I get in very high places. I discovered later that the cliff goes down thousands of feet to the valley below where the rapids tumble through gorges all over with moss and bracken and ancient trees.

We arrived at the cottage about a half hour after the pit stop. We'd passed through a little village that looked like it had come right out of *ye olde merrie* except for the few tourist shops and McDonalds.

We're down at the very end of Baton Lane, last place before the drop, just across the forest from the dairy. The drive in is along a track crowded on either side with huge pines and maples and silver birch, the last two doing their amazing red and gold color thing. I had the window rolled right down on the way in and the whole place smelled like heaven.

The cottage has got the power on to the house but the toilet's out back in a weather-beaten cloister with a make-shift door, and the bathroom is off the side of the house, like someone forgot it when they originally built the place. It's got a big old enamel bath, but no shower and we fire up a wood-chip stove to heat the water.

We've got verandahs all around the house and you can't get to any of the bedrooms from the inside – got to come out the kitchen and walk around the verandah. The heart of the cottage is that kitchen but the living room's its soul – it's in the center of every room, with the inner walls of the three bedrooms backing onto it, the fourth wall gracing an enormous fire-place that shares its chimney, and a doorway, with the kitchen. We keep the fire burning in there all day and all night against the mountain chill – it keeps the bedrooms warm as well. I guess if I'm going to be somewhere cold this time of year then here's the best place ever.

The gigs up here are terrific. Seems like everyone from anywhere around the mountain, or from down in the valley, have come to dance and drink while we play. Wally's the owner of the pub and he's been like Mr. Red Carpet since we tried out for him. Food and drinks have all been on the house each night we've played. The place has been packed and there hasn't been one rude comment about the way we look.

I've played with lots of bands over time and some of them have been really good, but they were never family and they didn't have the draíocht and I'd never stopped yearning to belong.

I don't know if I'll be with Fianna once we join Trevor next spring but Willie's pretty certain that two bodhrán players are going to be better than one. And all that aside, he'd said mischievously, who else'd have you? So, my heart's not breaking at the prospect of having to leave.

I've talked for hours – days – with Brighid, about what she calls "the gift" and how to work with it. Finally.

See since I was a boy I've seen what I figured were ghosts. Seen 'em everywhere. And it seems I spent most of my childhood thinking this was normal.

I remember when I was about five or six, something like that, having a conversation with this woman whose name was Alison. My mother hadn't long been with her new boyfriend Jeff and she was pregnant with Tracy already, but they'd decided not to cancel the summer holiday that we'd booked earlier.

We were staying in this old beachside house that we'd rented for two weeks. I was out in the yard when Alison had come out the back door and over to where I was lying on my stomach watching lizards fighting like real dinosaurs. She'd said it was nice that we'd come to stay with her; that she was on her own the rest of the year until the summer visitors came. She'd thought her son Rick must have made the arrangements – she never sees him anymore and she's sad about that.

We were chatting about all the things I could do during the holidays when my mother came out from the house and asked me who I thought I was talking to.

'This is Alison,' I introduced. Mum just kinda looked at me funny and ignored Alison and told me to come inside for lunch. I told Alison I'd maybe see to her soon. She just smiled at me and looked over to my mother's receding back.

Later that night I overheard my mother talking to her boyfriend and telling him that I had an imaginary friend.

I was really confused.

Over the years there were hundreds of them, and I realized that no one else besides me could see or hear them. That was scary, but I figured that everybody's different and that other people must see other things that I couldn't see. Some of the ghosts were nice and some were horrible, and some were sad, or frightened. Each of them had a story to tell me.

By the time I was twelve years old my mother had me to a

psychiatrist and he'd asked me lots of questions – mostly stupid – about how I'd felt when my dad left, as if I could remember, and about my mother and her boyfriend and Tracy, my little sister. I told him they were cool. Everything was cool. No problem. Nothing wrong. Nothing bothering me. He never shut up looking to find shit. Asked lots of questions about the people I "thought" I saw.

'N-no,' I'd said stammering. None of his business. I lied about them because I knew he was trouble. Prescribed these pills I was supposed to take to make the ghosts go away and make me feel better, like I didn't feel fine – just crowded.

Well, I took the pills for a while just to get everybody off my back. They didn't do anything, and I was still getting the people coming and still hearing their stories so in the end I just pretended to take them to make my mother happy, and so I wouldn't have to see that stupid doctor anymore.

And I stopped talking so I wouldn't stutter anymore. Hardly said anything other than yes, no, please, thank you, maybe and yeah okay, for about a year.

Then my mother's best friend from when she was at school came to visit.

Julie.

She'd been living in Paris, and studying music the last few years. That first night she stayed she'd played a recording of a band called The Chieftains. My whole world stopped. I asked her to play it again when it finished, and again when it was over the second time. She'd laughed that big open-mouthed laugh that I'll love 'til the day,
sometime in the ancient future, when I maybe die.

I think I fell in love for the first time. She had this crop of short, fire-engine red hair and eyes like forests and a cute mouth with an overbite. She was all dance and song and laughter.

She stayed a week and played me variations of the same kind of music, and talked about the lyrics and the style and the instruments.

She had a tin whistle and a flute and a bodhrán.

When she went away – and left me with a broken heart – I fell in love again. With poetry and the legends of Fionn MacCumhaill and the tales of the Red Branch and the secret of what the word Mórrígan really means, with Breo-saighit, that some call Brigid, and the high kings of Teamhair, and the Tuatha Dé Danann and the music – oh, the music!

I wrote to Julie, like she was my religion, for the whole of the following year and then, one day just like today but windier and city, this stranger comes to our door.

My mother answers the knock and there's this tall, lean guy with black hair all shaven across the front of his head and braided everywhere else, pale skin, grey eyes, all dressed in black, with a little silver harp earring hanging from one ear.

My mother's all suspicious until he tells her that Julie sent him to me.

Mum shows him into the apartment, still wary. He comes right on over toward where I'm sitting with my book abandoned, all curiosity at my visitor. I stand up as he approaches, and he holds out his empty hand and shakes mine vigorously.

'You staying around here?' asks my mother.

'Not far,' he replies.

'You here for long?' she asks.

'I'm here for Alan,' he answers, unsmilingly.

'Hmm,' she says. 'Can I get you something?'

'Water,' he says.

'Well, I'll be right back.' She sounds really on edge when all I am is excited.

He's got this big round package tucked in his other arm. We sit on the floor, and he holds it out to me.

'Julie sent you this,' he says. I touch the brown paper wrapper with reverence.

'Well open it, Sunshine.' There's laughter in his eyes.

I undo the string, already knowing from the shape of it what's inside.

Raven comes around just on twilight each night. He brings his own bodhrán with him and teaches me. He's really patient, 'cause I figure I'm never going to get the hang of it and 'cause every time I go to ask a question my stutter's really bad. He tells me I'm doing fine.

Some nights the room's crammed with ghosts but they're mostly there to listen. I work hard at not looking at them but Raven pipes up with 'It's like bloody Grand Central Station in here, man.'

'You can see 'em?' I ask incredulous.

'Nah, just sense 'em,' and he simply continues the lesson.

He's the one that starts telling me about the magic. He calls it the draíocht.

Then one night after several weeks he doesn't come. That's okay, I guess.

But then the next night he doesn't show up either and I'm really scared I've lost my only friend.

The following day the post drops off a thick brown envelope with my name on it, postmarked from somewhere not here. I get that kinda sick feeling when I touch it, knowing it's from him and knowing I'm not going to be happy about it.

Inside is a beat up thin stack of papers stapled together with *Thomas the Rymer* written on the cover and a note from Raven saying sorry he didn't get to explain but that we'd meet up again down the track.

My mother came into my room. I was fighting hard not to cry but she said it was a good thing really, 'cause he'd been such a weirdo and she'd never trusted him and that she and Jeff had thought about not letting him come anymore anyway as they were always on edge when he was around, especially with the two of us up here on our own together.

That night I shoved a few things into my backpack, put *Thomas the Rymer* into my coat pocket and the bodhrán into its cloth bag and climbed out of the window. I left my mother a note that was quite polite really, explaining that I just couldn't do it the way people seemed to think I should.

I never went back but I phoned occasionally. Until one time, when I called, the person on the other end of the line said they'd just moved in a month ago, and no, they didn't know about the previous tenants, and so now I don't know where they are anyway.

I took to living off the streets. For a while I stayed in the squats, but I was mostly freaked-out by the people who lived there and wasn't liking the way things got after dark. Place was full of ghosts, mostly in such a state of tragedy that I was suffocated by them. So, I made myself quite a good shelter in the park down by the memorial and I started busking during the day.

I eventually discovered the municipal library and used to spend hours there reading everything from myths and legends and books on paranormal phenomenon and poetry to witchcraft and other books that were maybe about the draíocht. The witchcraft stuff was the most familiar – like all these people here and now working with the spirits of the land and honoring the legends and the old ways and the sky and the waters and god and goddess that are living things from forever and not some pasty dead judgment like we used to get fed when I was in school. I figured I was one of them and started doing my own secret rituals down under the bridge by the canal.

Pat at the library used to lock up after me whenever I was there at closing time, which was most nights. In the end she let me stay and use the utilities room to bunk down in, telling me how much trouble she'd get into if I didn't do the right thing by her.

That summer I'd started using a deck of tarot to make a bit of extra money from the tourists. There was a market in the east end of town every Saturday and I'd spread out a cloth on the ground and try looking intensely mystical. I had a few people on the first day, out for a bit of a laugh and being skeptical because I was so young, but I brazened it out, stammer and all.

Thing was, each of them brought the shadow of their lives, or their own ghosts, with them and so when I talked to the people I said a lot of stuff that I got from them, not the cards.

The weeks after that there was always this queue waiting to get to me. I didn't charge a lot of money, but I was eating.

On weekdays I was busking with the bodhrán. Sometimes others'd join me with the fiddle or a whistle or a guitar and we'd do pretty-well just jamming.

Then I met Riley Dougherty who'd stopped to listen. He had a pub down on the south side and said it was called Mary Dooly's Tavern and that lots of bands playing traditional folk music worked there Thursday and Saturday nights and that I ought to think about coming over and maybe getting in on some gigs.

So I did.

Always played filler though – tough to get in. Most bands were used to playing together, and I was just too used to being a loner to even consider the hard work of starting up my own combo.

The last Saturday before the Summer Solstice and we're almost finished the first set when I see Raven over at the bar. He's grinning madly. Can't tell you how I got through that set without a mistake.

Came the break and I'm shoving people out of the way and grabbing him like a life raft and he's chuckling and hugging me back.

When I finally let go he sits back down on his stool and takes a gulp from his pint. 'You've improved,' he says with a twinkle in his eye.

'Where've you been,' I yell over the crowd.

'Doesn't matter,' he replies casually. 'What're you doing after the gig?'

'No plans,' I answer, knowing I never really have any anyway.

'You feel like traveling?' he asks.

'Where to?'

'Meet up with some folk at a high summer gathering,' he replies mysteriously.

I hear the thuk, thuk of the wood-splitter and figure Hunter and Matt are back from the forest with a load. Brighid and Rowan are cutting up root vegetables to go into the oven for the feast later and Hunter's lady, Puck, is outside brushing the honey and herb baste onto the wild goat that Hunter and Annis tracked down with Hunter's compound earlier in the day. Robin, who just turned four, is sitting up on a chair beside me 'reading' to me, out of his little pop-up book. Some story that's not written down.

Dylan's gone off to look for wild mint to add to the greens and Willie's sitting up next to the stove playing his fiddle. Raven went off in the bus to get some mead and ale from the pub in town.

Since taking the Quicken brew all my senses have honed. I can see further, I can hear in a way I figure a hound might; touch is so much sweeter than it ever used to be; food's amazing – but the nose is the best bit. I walk out into the misty garden. Wood-smoke and roasting meat and damp undergrowth and old pine trees and the ancient rock that's all around the place. And nothing's ever smelled so good. And nothing's ever felt so right.

Brighid told me and the others where the Fianna are going after the feast tonight. Heading to New Rathmore for the winter. They said they'd be taking us if we were willing (as if). This'll be the first time I've traveled there outside of my imagination.

It's very late. The sky is huge and black and moonless, glittering with stars and frost. We're all out around the remnants of the feast and the fire's down to embers. Brighid lays out the offering of food for the creatures of the forest as Hunter and Puck share the last of the mead with the rest of us, and pour some to the earth in a blessing of the land.

Everyone waits, in quiet excitement, as Hunter raises the ancient horn to his lips...

10

SEEING IN THE DARK

HEALING

*The word shaman, originating from the Tungus people of Siberia,
It means one who sees in the dark.*

INTRODUCTION

ALL CREATIVE PEOPLE I HAVE ever met are edge-dwellers. Living high up on the clifftop of mythworld. Overlooking a vast, seemingly bottomless depths. Many have fallen or jumped. Being witch is like that, because being witch is a way of living that requires we pay attention to what the gods are explaining. If we don't listen, we break. If we try to stay the same instead of shedding a skin we cannot see but only feel, we break. Today I sat with a person living on that edge. It took a while for this meeting to happen, and right at their first Saturn Return. How trapped by love, how dreadfully harmed by carelessness,
how vital and intelligent. Willing to learn.

Initiation | A Memoir: says:

Initiation is a mapped and charted experience that many people do not understand or know when the experience is not on their terms. You will be woken up. When wolf-mother takes us in her jaws and pulls us into the myth we are helpless. Myth is not fallacy. Myth is as real as the skin that keeps our rawness clothed. Myth is story without the author being known.

In explaining initiation Joseph Campbell, in Hero with a Thousand Faces, *tells us firstly of a* **threshold**. *We die to who we have been. And yes, always tragically. We cross into the* **liminal** *world and become lost. This could last a lifetime if we lack the necessary insight as to what is happening. We need to be on the lookout then, as we travel the days and nights of desolation and confusion, for the signs of the Return. We must keep our ears pricked and our tails bushy. There must be a Return. Someone to know us. To be met and the purpose of this new life be revealed.*

If we eventually become consciously that the place in which we currently live as the liminal world of not-life we may very well be ready to return. We will know. We will meet the **gatekeeper***. This could be someone already known to you, or someone new. They will* **complement** *the true you. This is not like any other compliment. The seeker is recognized for the depth of them and how far they have climbed from that pit. Words will liberate the dark night of the soul. The* **gatekeeper** *gives the keys to a new life. Do we have the guts to walk through? To accept the change with only courage? To leave that lost place, savage forest, mist of futility, cave of self-doubt and take the challenge of being raw, temporarily blind and furless?*

No one can hold us should we choose to make this choice, to wear the next mask and to clothe ourselves in this new garment of self. We don't have to cleave to the identity that we thought defined us. Life is art. Life wants experience through who we are and what we do. Wants the lone wolf to run with the pack.

A *level of insight* is a profound thing. Witching is kin to the work of shamanism. It's not the same because I am not Tungus and therefore that experience would be misappropriation. The following story was written as a way healing from the disability of soul loss. And every serious trauma tears us. Becoming whole in a society that is careless with both love and honesty can take a *lot* of work and insight. The following story illustrates the search for a ravaged identity and a broken-off piece of soul.

LOST SOUL STORY

THE PRE-DAWN LIGHT DAPPLES PATTERNS ONTO every surface of my room and the branches of the apple tree just outside the window break the silver of it into uncountable, thin-limbed marionettes.

Everywhere is the pale and dark greys of doves and pigeons. I sigh with the relief of its gentleness.

Morning slides in increments across the plank floor and I need to lay beneath the blankets for just a little while longer, to observe and to breathe this perfect air.

The redolence of wood smoke lingers from where the backed-up chimney returned it to the room last night as though to say, See? There are consequences to everything you do, but there are also consequences to what you don't do.

That slight, bitter, left-over scent of smoke, the merest hint of varnish that still breathed from the abandoned tins lined up along the back shelves along with rusting things and a manual I cannot read.

Caulking, tar, old wood. A history of barnacles. Salt air, the cool of the sea, my own hair, the tang of iron from the slow combustion stove, dusty rugs. The smell of an owl's regurgitated pellet that has eluded my hunt. The thatch of the roof and, oh, the merest signature of kelp.

For a moment a bubble of memory floats to the surface of my privacy and my stillness, but I burst it easily. Her face. That's why I am here. That's why I fled from that other place that once seemed so real but that became an abandonment of trust.

To learn to live without her.

When I have supped well upon the aroma of dawn I throw back the covers, pull on my jeans and the thick jumper that Mme. Bisset knitted and sold to me for a jar of my shells.

"Comment ça va, cherie?" she always says to me, her mouth expressing the syllables carefully in case I misunderstand her.

The people in the village think I am deaf and mute. They are tender because of it and they take my gifts seriously because I have become their superstition. The season the dark-haired girl moved into the old Pattenaude boatshed had been different. It was said that perhaps she was a selkie, washed up on the tide, her sleek furred skin buried deep within some hidden cave. That her first language was seal. They do not understand that I am a ghost.

M. Didier and his seven sons, who run the fishing boat, chasing the herring, had seen the smoke from my chimney on my first night here. The next day I saw the women in scarves, the children whispering behind their hands, astride their bicycles, watching.

From that day events in and around the village became noticeably different. The lambs were fatter that spring, the ewe's milk yielded richer curd. The rain was softer, and the bread rose higher. The flowers' colors were brighter and Sylvia and René Thierry, who had tried, and failed for so long, conceived a daughter, born healthy and rosy exactly nine months later.

People who have lived generations in the same place must, of course, notice when things are an anomaly. I cannot. I have moved around so often in my life that I am trackless, not even in the company of other gypsies.

I pull on thick socks and sturdy boots. I go to the stove, add kindling to the still-smoldering back log and wait for the eruption of flame. I feed it more sustainable fuel before taking up my bucket and unlatching the door.

Oh! Oh! Everywhere is soft with mist. It is like white and grey are lovers. I can just see the winking of light, like excited diamonds, on the still and silent sea half a mile away along the barren beach.

The air smells even more delightful out here. The sounds of small things in the underbrush and the *peewit* of the curlews in the distance only add to the recipe, the muffled calls of gulls and the labored *chu, chu, chu* of a motor informing me that M. Didier's boat is heading for the shore with its hold full. Then, beneath it all, like the sigh of my young years at the kiss of that boy, the almost indistinct susurration of the sea on the shingle and sand and uncountable tiny shells at the water's edge.

I fill my bucket from the tap at the well beside the apple tree.

I leave the door open when I come back inside so that the day does not feel neglected. It accepts my welcome.

The last of the lengths of timber that once supported boats for repair in this shed—my home—are stacked beside the stove alongside my axe and the small logs it has split. Those logs had been piled high against the outside wall, a mysterious gift, delivered by some anonymous benefactor one day while I was in the village, along with the axe. I sent kisses their way.

I use the thick beams, their nails driven deep on one side, dangerously spiked on the other, interspersed with the logs. The smell is resinous, redolent with memory. They don't mind that I am the catalyst to their transition. They had been idle a long time. Enough to cause cramp, thought one. Wood can be funny.

They understood, inherently, that as ash they will feed the garden and so become the food I eat that is shared with not too many rabbits, and owls that hunt for mice which in turn scavenge for seed.

The apple tree is ponderous with fruit because of that ash. We have thought well of one another and I have stroked its ancient trunk and rested my head to listen, knowing the old are often forgotten young women with stars in their eyes who believed in love, or once-dashing young men who were witty and charming but who then went to war only to come back in silence. That their stories are considered inconsequential because they are wrinkled is savagely wrong.

This tree is a little in love with me. I am honored. I will never ignore it and I will never take its love for granted.

I shall make apple jam and apple sauce and preserve some and gesture to M. Giroud, asking if I might be allowed the use of his pressoir to make cider.

M. Giroud has an orchard of many fruits that he sells at the market every Monday. He also has his own restaurant that tourists love because he cooks traditional Breton cuisine. His is the only restaurant in the village just as Mme. de Villier has the only patisserie. Mr. Monkton, an English expat who adores everything French, took over the boucherie after Jean Matis, its previous occupant, killed himself the day after the funeral of his lifetime partner, Henri, who had finally succumbed to AIDS. It had been with him since the wildness of his Parisian youth, but he had been kept alive for years by the love of Jean and an ever-improving medicine that just wasn't quick enough.

I can understand why Jean Matis did it. Life does not have to be suffered. It is just as fine to become earth. He had no one else.

While I wait for the kettle to boil to make tea I check up on my treasures that line the window sill and that form a spiral on the floor that I must walk, each evening at sunset, with my candle lit, seeking the center. It is the safest place in the world. I do not need to sit there for hours but for just enough time for it to matter. I would not presume upon the center for too long.

It is also the heart of the world and that is where I will be remembered.

Much of my time is taken with finding these treasures. Certain shells. This piece of bone—like white wood with simply no weight to it at all—that could have come from Guinea, or Alaska, or New Zealand and whose identity and predictability have long since been given to the ocean in sacrament.

I open the window and pull up the covers of my bed and fluff the pillow and that is my work done.

I wash my face.

I tie back my hair.

After my tea I shall ride my bike into the village. Mme. de Villier likes the treasures I choose for her as much as M. Giroud. I can, now, also take them both fennel and lemon verbena as both have become monsters in my garden and the other herbs and vegetables have requested I disseminate the offenders. To which the fennel and lemon verbena have agreed apologetically.

Mme. de Villier makes a pain du jour especially for me every third day, and she also gives me butter, and a fat slab of cheese, because she does not consider life civilized without good cheese.

I have not spoken since I arrived here, and I do not know how long I have been here. Perhaps I am an illusion. and nothing is real.

. . .

Minnie Temple had no idea she had been deserted by her own soul. She had no idea why there was a shadow, like her grandfather's cutthroat razor, slicing off the edges of her mind.

She was a strong woman. She had raised her children on her own. She was an achiever.

Aspiring writers paid for her advice and freelance editing, a willing participant in hope.

She'd lived in Dalton until a few months before, the community that sat like an expensive jewel, nestled within the crescent shore of a white, sandy beach. A paradise, bathed in sunlight like bleached gold, drenched in the scents of frangipani and butterfly ginger, was her home.

Behind the town were the highlands where the pink buds on the monumental cedars used to touch the sky. Before they were all cut down. That was long ago, though, long before Minnie moved from the city, but who knows where the ghosts of the dead go, if they go anywhere at all?

Life was good for Minnie. Then why this anxiety?

Ignore it.

She ignored it all the time. Pushed it aside.

She had recently moved from the house in Dalton, that she had called home for over a decade, to those very same mountains that once grew the cedar. It had only been a rental. Minnie didn't believe in mortgages. She said the bank owned them, really, and you never could do whatever you wanted. And what's ownership anyway, other than a First World construct of permanence in the face of the elephant in the room? No. She moved from that house with, almost, no backward glance as backward glances were dangerous. She let the things she'd buried there stay buried.

Minnie sat at the window of her study working on her most recent screenplay. A comedy, despite the growing darkness within her.

That's the way of writers: things, memories and objects, snippets of conversation, personal experiences, history, love, betrayal, the lies of governments and their fathers. Like *String Theory*, each thread a doorway to a possible dimension from where the next story would manifest.

An hour later and Minnie was satisfied. She saved her work and remembered to back it up this time.

Coffee, she thought.

Then it occurred to her that perhaps she should stop drinking coffee. Maybe that was the cause of the anxiety. She only drank one or two cups a day but perhaps her adrenals needed a rest.

Minnie was dying—not her body, no, the essence of who she was—and it never occurred to her. Just a kind of shaking shriveling that began at her core and worked its way to the surface.

It began with the night of the twenty fifth of September and what undid her were the sounds of cows in utter despair. Hundreds of them. Minnie would be hard pressed to describe, that: the high-pitched moo—like a howl, throats hoarse with desperation—of mothers searching and searching but never finding their children. The Holocaust came to her mind, and Wounded Knee.

Of course, Minnie did not sleep. It reminded her of the time her son was bullied, and she could do nothing. She remembered all the times she thought she could keep her offspring safe. She never could.

Even though she'd lived in Dalton for over a decade she's never been away from the coast until now. She didn't know the baby cattle were removed from their mothers before either was ready. She wasn't prepared for the rising panic and empathy.

Minnie had a coffee date with friends in town the following morning at a cafe, at ten thirty.

She grabbed her keys and bag and phone and locked the door of the renovated Queenslander that she rented from an old friend. A man she trusted. Someone who wanted her there.

Once down the mountain and onto the flat of the farming country she gunned the accelerator and the old Beamer purred towards the two-lane turnoff at the T intersection.

She pulled over to the left, her indicator informing the flatbed pick-up behind her of her intention. She stopped at the stop sign.

A cattle truck pulled up to the right of her and Minnie made the mistake of turning in its direction. The sides of the truck were lined with wide horizontal wooden slabs. Between them was about a six-inch gap. And looking through it were the faces and the eyes of the children that had been taken from their mothers. And they were all silent. And they were looking at her.

Minnie had a fascination with Auschwitz, with Buchenwald. She remembered seeing archival footage of Jews being loaded into cattle trucks, mothers in fine wool coats with silver fox fur collars, men in tailored overcoats, children in gloves, all looking at the camera in passing and the wide shots, of Nazis in svelte black uniforms and shiny black boots, sporting riding crops or rifles and with Lugers in elegant, leather holsters.

Where are we going?

The baby cattle were thinking that perhaps this was some silly game and that they'd be back frolicking and gamboling in the paddock by late afternoon, the temporary loss of mother and milk a faded memory.

Minnie sat. Paralyzed.

The truck pulled away, the eyes still following her, the pickup behind her blaring its horn, before tearing past, the driver yelling something like *ar, ya marin' garra wukin da*, that Minnie didn't attempt to interpret.

That night the rains came, and Minnie's vegetable garden flooded to death.

The following morning, the property owner—her friend—knocked on her door and asked whether there was a coffee to be had.

Sure, said Minnie.

She fixed them both espressos in little white cups and they sat at the kitchen table.

I'm selling up, he said, sipping.

Minnie didn't show a thing.

Oh?

Really sorry. I know I said you'd be here as long as you wanted but, fuck, what am I going to do? Whipper snipper for the rest of my life?

Oh, Minnie said. How long do I have?

At least three months, I reckon. You alright? You don't look so good.

I'm fine, Minnie lied, looking out over a panorama that should have been beautiful but that was too full of that wet, endless grey.

She carried on with her work and she fed the cat; the last of a long line of now-dead pets. The last responsibility in her life. It didn't matter. Did it? That she had to relocate again?

Then one day, driving home from town, she got to the base of the foothills. She could no more drive up it than eat her own hand. Minnie was broken.

She eventually drove to her doctor's surgery in Dalton, walked in and whispered to the receptionist that she wouldn't make it to the end of the day if he couldn't fit her in.

He put her on anti-depressants right away.

That metaphorical grandfather's cutthroat razor, though, had severed her from herself and Minnie, damaged and desperate, was determined to find herself but the only place she could do that was to look within. What she found was a gaping, ragged wound where her identity used to be. Minnie went through the wound and began to hunt.

I am a ghost—no, a voyeur. Is this my imagination? I'm in a large, dilapidated old boatshed and an ageless, pretty woman sits at the table.

Go away, she says, almost imperceptibly.

I'm confused because I don't know why I am here. What I am in this place. What I am doing here. In this sparsely-furnished, old wooden shack. And then realization strikes. I am air.

Beneath me is a spiral made up of shells and pieces of glass worn smooth by the sea, bleached bird bones, thin, flute-like pieces of white driftwood. It is heart-wrenchingly beautiful. It reminds me of younger days; of wandering the dunes, alone, along a childhood shoreline, and not thinking.

I live here now, she says. I won't come back. You can't make me.

I know who she is.

We are one person. I need you, I whisper. Come back. Please?

I can't. I loved you, and you betrayed me.

How?

You were busy being important.

I'm here now.

It's too late. I don't trust you.

Help me. I want to understand.

Help you? Leave me alone. I am loved here.

Then I hear the silence. In long intervals between the piping of curlews, the ack-ack of plovers and the distant call of gulls. I feel how cool the air is and notice how delicate the light.

I'm falling to pieces, I admit.

And you don't know why? she accuses. Do you remember burying the dogs? Them like brothers? All the others? Losing the house that was home?

Mourn, she yelled.

Dear god, I think, fleeing back to my body, and weeping like I have never let myself before.

I don't know if I'll ever get over this. Ever be whole. I don't know if I'll have to haunt her until I die of emptiness for love of her and this terror of living broken.

11

PALEFACE

FOR YOUR COVEN

IN 1978, ON A JOURNEY TO LONDON, I SAT ON A plane in Beirut airport with a gun in my face for an hour. War raged in Lebanon. The people that could, fled. To refuge. For themselves and their children. To live. They came here. They were not welcomed.

My family is descended from ancient tribal people and many of us know who they are. The gods they are before the asphalt and concrete. The hidden seeds of the first forests. Co-species beyond recall.

Do you know? Do you care? Or are you trapped within the shallow lands, the ravaged landscape. Huge cranes. Metal girders. The neon and plastic and irradiation of the current, seemingly senseless, century? My veins are blue with ancestral blood. I am shamed by colonial arrogance wherever it has bludgeoned, with its canons, its broken treaties and its religion. But when I tell you I re-member what is that to you? A forgotten people relegated to the past tense? No. Still here. If I tell you I am a *Twa Corbies* woman, am I speaking of difference?

Yes.

All stories are different, or they would be boring. A monocrop is the grief of earth who would revel in diversity and sigh with delight. Are you still reading this? Or have you gone off to explore what the word means before you go on. I smile if you have done so because now we can meet.

I can also hear your story.

I sat in Beirut airport with that semi-automatic rifle pointed at my face, and my seven year old son, beside me, said, Mummy, are we safe? I smiled at the soldier and he smiled back.

Yes, I said. They are just scared.

War raged in Lebanon. Lebanon is the shore of the Phoenician people. One of the greatest seafarers and explorers in the known history of humans. The people who gave us our alphabet. The history books would tell us that the war was civil. Sectarian. But I am ashamed to say I have not sat at dinner with one Lebanese refugee and asked them for the truth.

As I wrote at the start of this grimoire, I am Briton. I am also Connacht, Albanach, Parisi, Breton and a little bit Viking. These cultures are deep in the song-bones of those of us descended. Our language somewhat lost but pocketed in Cymraeg or in Gaeilge. Our traditions tattled about by old men in universities guessing and considering us vulgar in comparison to our conquerors. Our stories inked in prejudice by monks.

I was a presenter at the Byron Spirit Festival in 2015, along with Nila Chandra and Matty Connolly. We were there to take a bunch of participants through a two-day, concentrated version of the book, *Priteni*, and the experience was called *Blue People*. That is because, as Tacitus wrote, apart from our tattoos (that he thought was paint) we cover our bodies with fat, tinted with the blue of woad, for night hunting. Hopefully this would be, for those attending, a visceral trance, hypnotic experience. I'd been invited by Kate Little, one of the organizers. Kate also asked me to sit on the panel of indigenous elders, to tell them of these massacred and defeated ancestors of ours.

I was the only light-skinned person on that panel. The only woman. I felt like a fraud. I said that to the gathered audience, then I assured them I was not. I don't know if they believed me, and I really didn't care. There are rafts of revivalist faux-Celts who might not be. Or might be. Why not really find out? And then share that knowledge with the people who don't? With no lore. The other elders were Hawaiian, Maori and three mob from different countries of this land. What did they see when they looked out at the crowd? A bunch of sun-browned people, swaying to the music in exotic tribal clothing, while my colleagues' aunties endure dialysis? Whose incarceration rate is over the top, still, even after a Royal Commission into Aboriginal Deaths in Custody, in 1991 made recommendations that today, in the pale pre-dawn of 2018 are yet to be implemented? In most countries indigenous voices are still silenced while neopagans crow the names of deities they've been told represent them. Without knowing that they do not exist. Well not as the populist media, and archetypal enthusiasts would
tell us that they do.

I didn't chatter on, at that gathering of elders, about by own heritage, but rather told the story of that gun and a meeting of heart:

One day I walked along Spencer Street in Melbourne and two young men, of seeming-Lebanese heritage, walked towards me. One had a teardrop tattooed under one eye. I'm not naïve. I know what it means. That was beside the point. I also knew what their parents had endured, losing their homeland and about intergenerational trauma. They stopped when they saw me. I put my hand to my heart because in 1978 I'd sat in Beirut airport with a gun in my face, because war raged on their once proud and beautiful streets, and I could see that in him. Both men raised their hands to their hearts. Their eyes to the tattoo on my face. They knew. We met. We said nothing but as I passed him I touched his face.

The Cronulla riot happened over a decade ago as I write. All those young white Anglo, faces, with Australian flags draped over their naff shoulders, that means nothing. As though this island was theirs, when it is not. As though they know who they are, when they do not. Do any of them know why the Irish call the Union Jack the *Butcher's Apron*? No. And I do not decry the young. They are tomorrow's ideologies and hard workers. But if they had been in Beirut airport with a gun in their faces in 1978; when war raged in Lebanon, they might have asked for the stories of that savage war. Of the neglect of the people of this land to truly embrace those so cruelly ravaged. Even
now, those men idle their hope away, neglected on Manus Island, forgotten and afraid. If we'd known the stories of the parents of those

Lebanese refugees, there would have been no riot because storytelling is as old as us. Lore is how we learn. From before there was the written word. Non-literate people are insulted when they are branded illiterate.

Several days prior to the above experience with the festival, and the elders panel, I sat with Alison, the festival's promotions person, at the Rock and Roll café in Mullumbimby. She didn't have any prior knowledge of what we were presenting so it was, initially, awkward. We were about half an hour into the interview when a tall, narrow, jolly man joined us.

So, he says, you're Ly?

Hi, yes, and you are?

I'm one of the directors of the festival. So, Blue People!

Yes.

Is this some Hindu thing?

Do I look Hindu? Why would you think that?

Um. Because their gods are blue?

Would you excuse us? I need to finish up here with Alison.

You asking me to leave?

I turned to Alison and asked her to remind me where we were up to.

So, when I tell you I that I am a whole lot of Erin and Alba, and a little

bit Norse, what is that to you? I am a paleface, but don't call me white. That is an insult. What it implies is in difference to everybody else.

12

SOMETIMES THERE ARE REASONS FOR BEING ANONYMOUS AND LOST

FOR YOUR COVEN

AND WHEN WE ARE ANONYMOUS AND LOST we all tend to invent ourselves. When we do not have a mirror or an ancient story to hear and know to be true. When we make trouble, when we don't do what society demands, when we don't behave in an appropriate way we're going to be subject to criticism. Be warned. You and I might be thought of as ornery, or pig-headed or even somewhat arrogant. A fool. A freak or a piece of work. But what about when that's an insult because it is simply untrue, and others choose to see the world through other eyes?

One way of living with being anonymous and lost happens because there is no one to offer us true stories.

One way is to become sullen. Resentful. Or work like crazy *to* fit in. I understand that. Loneliness is the way of the edge-dweller. But I must say that even though this is a track through the forest that myth suggests drove Merlin mad, it is not the path only trodden deep by deer, but wolves in hunt of deer. Because there comes a time when the pretense is like an old otter skin hanging on the back of the kitchen door that used to belong to a selkie (who abandoned it long ago). It smells of rot. And that's what'll happen to the person in this one thing.

> *Stories instantaneously bypass the ego. The ego cannot absorb the entire pith of story. The story as a form of entertainment. While the ego is kept happy, thinking it is being entertained, the soul and the spirit are listening deeply. The flow of images in stories is medicine—similar medicine to listening to the ocean or gazing at sunrises. No direct interaction has occurred—the ocean did not jump into your body and fill you. But there is something about seeing, hearing, and smelling the ocean that has bypassed the ego, and straightened out many things that were in disarray within the psyche.* --Dr. Clarissa Pinkola Estes

The other thing is to learn. Now, that can be a labyrinthine, maze-like endeavor, because not all information that passes itself off as knowledge, *is* knowledge. Much of it has been copied from the notes of another student. Right when the exam was on. And there's me thinking that person must have the right answers because I didn't understand that the study was open to questioning.

Despite the deceptions and the acceptances along the way, I became a gatherer. And I know many, many gatherers. Some are scholars and teachers, certainly, but the best amongst them are the storytellers, questioners and hunters. Modern interpreters of myth and spirituality. The challenger of what spirituality even means.

The center of the maze is what happens if we get there. It's the realization that hidden within everything we have learned just might be a *something*. But the center of this maze is an unborn child. A puppy still unlicked within a caul. An egg nestled deep within lore.

There it is then. There is no way to deal with this world as a person. People have been too often, and untruthfully, too much at the center. Not the myth and who we are with that. Myth is a story without an author. It's been passed through the generations like some legendary vine. And myth is also the soil in which the vine gains strength. From which all of us, who walk that edge and beg that cloud to rain on this desert of shallow verbiage, unfurls from seed to stem to root to bud to leaf to fruit.

I was no one. I was lost. I was a cinderblock tenement. An orphanage of abandonment. You know it, or you wouldn't still be reading. There are ropes around our wildness. Some are rough and cruel, yes, but some are silky and seemingly languid, and they are as intentional as chain.

Encountering indigenous lore, and learning the stories of the Samé (Norway), the legend of Sedna (Inuit), Cú Chullain and Scáthach (Ireland and Scotland), Na'ashjéii Asdzá (Navajo), Hinewhaitiri (Maori), the story of Bunjil (of the Kulin traditional custodians, where I currently rest my head at night) is to ask to know people within their ancestral landscapes. To understand that the landscapes *are* the people... and every rock and sparrow and chuckle-gurgling burn within it are also the people. Our deaths, our lives. But do these old stories hold relevance today?

> *The Anglo-Saxons had a word, geidd, to describe the intensities and beauties of language at its most transcendental, regardless of whether it was found in speech or on paper, in a fireside ballad or an epic saga recited in the longhouse. It was what they regarded as the true poetic spirit. The giedd is the delicious scent that Trickster seeks in this confluence of influence.*
>
> Dr Martin Shaw, A Branch from the Lightning Tree.

It is unwise to trust the way history is written. Or even what you believe is your own story. Challenge it. Ask who wrote it; who writes it because it is being invested every day anew. Consider whether the author might have been biased. Who wrote that Mórrigan is a battle goddess, when the one word is two words, and the word queen is not an Irish word… So, what are we talking about here? And was there war in Ireland or mere coup? For who has counted the dead? And if that landscape was represented by a person or a clan why did they fight? Who propaganda's the idea of warfare on another people when that is the language of empires, rape and broken treaties? When did sovereignty become human in difference to forest and mountain stream-gods; genius loci?

Do not accept the shallow writings of the person adding the same diatribe with some neo-pagan slant of their own. Bypass and seek humus.

But we must be strong, and we must walk knowingly. Earth has taken at least since the last Ice Age to create the depth in which deep ancestral roots thrive. If, in stupidity, we seek only to please ourselves and not be the landscape and the people of every species who are also the landscape we will have entered the illusion of fairyland. Will have drunk the drink and eaten the food and taken the gold, only to find it dust when we awaken.

"The relationship between thinking and walking is also grained deep into the language history, illuminated by perhaps the most wonderful etymology I know. The trail begins with our verb to learn, meaning to 'acquire knowledge'. Moving backwards in language time, we read the Old English leornian, 'to get knowledge', to be cultivated.' From leornian the path leads us further back, into the fricative thickets of Proto-Germanic, and to the word liznojan, which has a base sense of 'to follow or to find a track' (from the Proto-Indo-European prefix leis-, meaning 'track'). 'To learn' therefore means at root—at route—'to follow a track'. Who knew? Not I, and I am grateful for the etymologist-explorers who uncovered those lost trails connecting 'learning' with 'path-following'. Robert Macfarlane, The Old Ways.

13

HOW GOD KILLS THE WORLD

The Slander of Wilderness

CONTEMPLATION

INTRODUCTION

I DO NOT SEE THE REASON FOR REPLACING otter and acorn with broadband and cut and paste in the Oxford Junior Dictionary, whilst leaving the words religion, doctrine and dogma and god (the one that seems like an old man). Religion is but an organization that's credibility on the agreement of the invisible. On the whole religion bases its existence on the delusion of an omnipotent, male, eternal, righteous and supreme being[70]. Its adherents revile "Mother Nature" as some cruel and savage female entity when a cyclone takes out a coastal city or an earthquake undermines a nuclear power plant or, as ironically happened in Christchurch, New Zealand, in 2011, a cathedral. Twice.

---

[70] 1. (n) being 1. the state or fact of existing *"a painting gradually coming into being"* 2. A state of continued behaviour *"he is being a fool"* 3. A living thing

This contemplation does not intend to regale over the psychological subtleties of spires and miters, dressing in ornate gowns and caps, consuming the body of an historically suspect long dead man, daily or weekly, nor the asking of one person of another to believe this to be an absolute truth. Not at the necessity of bowing and the intonation of prayer at the insistence of bells or the taboos against women's menstrual flow, the cutting of genitals or the covering of the head in any other instance than to protect against elements. These are all rituals[71] and indoctrinated inheritances. I need to get their existence on paper as an example of unreason.

Mars: Roman.

Represented astrologically and metaphorically, also, by the planet Mars. Consensually thought of as an anthropomorphic deity of war.

How did that happen? I'll come back to that.

On the last day of March[72] 2017. Cyclone Debbie made landfall over the Whitsunday Island and the far north-east coast of Australia, destroying boats, houses, businesses, vehicles and infrastructure.

Debbie temporarily wounded electricity provision and other human necessities. The estimated cost, we are informed in news reports, is

---

[71] ritual, from 1. the Latin *ritualis*, meaning the proven way of doing a thing 2. Sanskrit *ṛtá*, in Vedic religion "the lawful and regular order of the normal, therefore proper, nature and true structure of cosmic, worldly, human and ritual events. The word *ritual* first recorded in English in 1570 and came into use in the 1600s to mean "the prescribed order of performing religious services" or more particularly a book of these prescriptions.
[72] On the Gregorian calendar

likely to be in the billions of dollars.

What is awry about the above paragraph is that cyclones have likely been of greater or lesser intensity over the countless millennia of indigenous human habitation in the same region and money was not an issue.

The above discussion does not include harm to other species. Relatives and co-beings on earth. It does not include the uncomfortable truth that the real inundation of these environments is people. That the viewpoint of disclosure is an androcentric myopic. That this viewpoint is considered absolute and authentic, and acceptable, to millions of readers or viewers or listeners of this truly mediocre story exposes us as brainwashed. Simply and erroneously aware only of the species of animal known as humanity.

Natural catastrophes seem to have increased over the past several decades, whether wildfires in California or the landslide in Nepal. I wonder whether these news events would have had an impact on our information-informed psyches if humanity did not figure so prominently in the telling. Sinkholes currently dotting the landscape of Siberia do not gain headline news. The rarity of one such, in Turkmenistan, is called the Door to Hell by local people due to constant eruption and flame. And Gozel Yazkulieva, a visitor from Ashgabat, said, "You immediately think of your sins and feel like praying."[73] Religious commentary on a phenomenon of such wildness. Not much was said of the culling of at least a quarter of a million reindeer in the north of that region due to an anthrax outbreak when

---

[73] Source: news.com.au June 22, 2014

the permafrost melted, revealing animals, dead from that disease in the past, and releasing it into the environment. That same permafrost melt is also releasing an unprecedented quantity of methane into earth's atmosphere[74]. You're not thinking, politicians.

In so many ways our current understanding of the world is based on the word—Logos—and since the invention of the camera on image. Visual impact. Some may, on reading this article thus far, think me crass and thoughtless, lacking human compassion. I am not. I feel deeply for those suffering the aftermath of earth's weather extremes. I also feel deeply for the current survivors of the trauma that is Aleppo, for those tortured by our own species in either the name of righteousness throughout history or just because sadism and the capacity for utter cruelty developed. I am horrified at the imposed starvation of millions of humans in Africa; that in 2015 more than ten million people suffered tuberculosis[75], the continuous and avalanching mental and physical malaise of us as a species, and that many of the sources I have cited here will vanish when the internet ceases to be. That we live in cities and cannot feed ourselves. That we overpopulate our mother and shred her of other life forms with vast mono-cropping and gouging. That we impose noise to the extent that we do. That in one city people bow their heads and shoulders over their mobile phones as though in obeisance while in another a mountain of garbage buries children alive.

We *can* stop it.

We can understand these and many other incidents historic,

---

[74] Source: *Review*, Climate change and the permafrost carbon feedback.
[75] *WHO*

current and probably future by changing firstly our perspective of earth and our correct mutual being, secondly by altering our language and commentaries both mentally and verbally, thirdly by acting on the previous two and lastly by realizing how what we have been taught is wrong (in the sense it is incorrect). We have been lied to and are continuing to be lied to, we lie to ourselves and our children and, unless we are stopped or stop we will continue to do so, removing the right to a life well lived from subsequent generations. Because we are at a tipping point.

The human impact on a globally-secured future is precarious. Brother and sister orangutan, rhinoceros, whale, wolf and elephant mutilated and slaughtered, and on the extinction's abyss, for the seeming benefit of the few. That bears should live in cages with tubes to their bile glands for the supposed erectile dysfunction of a few men offends me beyond words. That krill is now harvested as the newest trend in omega 3 oil for the health conscious—almost the sole food of the baleen whale—and that the trend in almond milk and soy products are stripping soil and water from earth, and killing those who seek to prevent the take—at an historically unprecedented rate should alarm anyone. The consumerist drive for countless unnecessary and non-recyclable products would be laughable if not so mortally wounding.

Technology, pharmaceuticals, weapons, poison and plastic.

For harm on such an abhorrent scale to be occurring in my lifetime is due to six things only: supply and demand. Greed and fear. Apathy and denial. What has snuck up on us, also, is the dehumanizing of our own species by the new language: the economy spoken of as a person, companies becoming persons, the roboticization of what were once human occupations and pastimes. Endemic loneliness as communities are torn apart by rampant development. Business or boredom. And constant distraction through multimedia.

As an addendum to this introduction I will add that it was explained to a younger and much more naïve me, many years ago, that news is entertainment. That, again, somebody profits from the extrapolation and exploitation of the misery, in the main, of the human dilemma.

MARS AND MITHRA
Soldiers' Deities

This contemplation began twixt sleeping and waking one morning. I have been editing a conversation with an American podcast for inclusion in an album of such conversations. The final discussion I edited before sleep last night was concerned the anthropomorphizing of the Pennines into a female, human-type deity that has been named Brighid. Misinterpreting indigenous understanding of this god through the countless generations' beliefs.

What if it's all wrong? What if it's all guesswork? Someone passed off a person as a supreme being and humanity bought into the lie and so taught each other this utter mass delusion. The clue is the word *God* or *Gods*. Even *Goddess/s*. With a capital letter. Fixing a perspective. The repetition of the word religion in every text recognizable to the known world and the concept of worship. The bilious overuse and excuse of the word sacrifice. Smiling saccharine politicians giving out tokens, called medals, to dead boys who knew such terror, and who died so deplorably in each recent war, while the men, with clean hands that sent them, call them retrospective heroes. And hide the ones thus maimed. Or the descendants of those affected by the bombs on Hiroshima and Nagasaki, the people of Maralinga's hundred and twenty-five-year curse, agent orange and dirty bombs.

The constant bombardment, of our remembered sense of a forest floor, humus, and silenced by statuary and symbolism: a tortured and mutilated dead man on a cross (so similar to Odin I try not to say anything), to that of Babylon and Egypt in deep animist time, Greece and Rome at the crossroads between animism and now, through to the ceiling of the Sistine chapel, the money-dripping Palace casino franchise, to the pizzazz of the latest iPhone, the weirdness of flawless teeth and the pillars of the American White House so very, intentionally Graeco-Roman. This contemplation is an attempt to let *you* off the hook. To allow *you* to opt out.

Those of you who study mythology or philosophy, or the humanities in general, will simply learn the same things as have been taught since the era of what is called the Classics, the study of mainly Greek and Roman literature and culture. Problem with that is that it is the epitome of classist elitism. A hierarchy of men.

No other creature gets a mention unless it serves the will of man.

From children born of men's thighs and out of the side of men's heads we are taught, oh yes, you can accept that. Studying the Classics[76] was, and still is, considered the study of the highest thought. Highest. There's another of those words. Adopted through the Middle Ages as the thing to learn. Still taught in universities. Pythagoras, Aristotle, Plato (I exclude the Cynics, although they remained in cities and begged. They didn't up and do anything productive like farm).

Of the country people we hear nothing. That they provided everything necessary from both their farming practices to the boar that graced the tables to the vineyards, that grew the grape. Nothing is said. Of the hunter of rabbit and deer, salmon and pigeon for the pie nothing is written. Of the bard, and the *draiocht*[77] of the druids, we must seek through thorns of bigotry. That until the mid-twentieth century a student was unable to learn the Classics without also being fluent in both Greek and Latin, that all the healing plants and herbs and poisons must also be known by a Latin name is indicative of the control that empires have held over subsequent empires right into the current era.

The Roman Empire enslaved entire populations and imposed its domination onto everyone. (Cyrus of Persia, whose warriors took the pants from the Hellenes, was a dynasty man.) Those that Rome could not control it murdered. And most of the lands and people they conquered did not bother with writing. Or statues. They had culture though. And thanks to Tacitus we have records of them albeit biased. Boats, cattle, gold, tin, copper, oak forests for ship building, jet,

---

[76] From the Latin classicus, meaning belonging to the highest class of citizens
[77] Gaelic: *magic*

diamonds. Oh, bit of a long list but they were barbarians[78] according to common consideration. What? Wrong again? Savages[79], is that a better term? No? No. Wrong again. Which *leader*, what government (corporation) of the known world, today, is any different?

So where is this going? The child was a foal, and his mother was of the wild herd, and the most profound thing that could ever be imagined was the moment the symbiosis, between human and horse, adapted into a mutual experience of each other. The same story is of a birth in a stable to a virgin[80]. The 'child' born in that 'stable' or cave, whether named Dionysus or Mithra or the later fictional character Joshua ben Miriam called Jesus, a christed man[81] is still that moment when the supposedly wild four-legged became our friend. I say supposedly because it is condescending, and therefore irresponsible, to assume wild/tame at all. We just are. But, we cause separation in our acquiescence to that idea. How do our brothers and sisters become tame? What? Like us? Are we tame? What does tame even mean?

---

[78] Latin barbarous, meaning different speech and customs
[79] Latin silva, meaning *of the woods*
[80] Barbara G. Walker documents in The Woman's Encyclopedia of Myths and Secrets, "Hebrew Gospels designated Mary by the word *almah*, mistakenly translated 'virgin,' but really meaning 'young woman."
[81] From the Gk cristos, meaning anointed, from the Hebrew *meshiyach*. The word meshiyach *is a derivation of the Egyptian word* messeh *and was the fat of the crocodile (sbk. or sobek) used to anoint a pharaoh, possibly as part of the embalming process, therefore consigning the being to eternal life (again a modern interpretation)* allegedly adopted by the Hebrews during their time spent in that territory (ca. 1250BCE). East African Arabs traditionally anointed themselves with lion's fat to gain courage and provoke fear in other animals. A technique of 'sympathetic magic', or more appropriately, because what does that mean, symbiosis between species. Animism.

Why do so many references to deities relate to the sun, in Mesopotamia, in Persia, in Anatolia, is because the Fertile Crescent is the womb of the grains of the future (I'm nowhere near Europe in this article because all modern religions began a long way from home. and I can't for the life of me think why. Oh. That's right. "By way of a hostile sword".[82]

For 2.5 million years humans fed themselves by gathering plants and hunting animals that lived and bred without their intervention. Homo erectus, Homo ergaster and the Neanderthals plucked wild figs and hunted wild sheep without deciding where fig trees would take root, in which meadow a herd of sheep would graze… Yuval Noah Harari, <u>Sapiens</u>.

---

[82] Bede

There, in the Mesopotamian Delta, where the Tigris and Euphrates Rivers meet, is where the eating of the seeds of grasses originated (with the exception, when recording the diets of people in the Americas, maize or corn). The Agricultural Revolution. Well not a revolution really. It hadn't happened before as far as we know. When considering the erection of astronomical architecture, from the great pyramid of Cheops, to the Callanish Stones on the Isle of Lewis, in the Outer Hebrides, knowledge of seasons of hunted species, the return of migrating birds, the precise era for the foraging of edible fungus--edible or hallucinogenic—and even the gathering of nuts would have depended on observation more of the sun than the moon. Whether hunter-gatherer, nomad, or relatively settled tribe, the earth's closeness or distance from the sun informs us of our dinner. Like the Polynesian seafarers who find an island in a trackless ocean because their wizard Hau Maka is asleep in the stern and dreams it, the knowledge of the seasons of hunger or plenty are who we are. It dwells like a sleeping mammoth in our DNA. When not interfered with it keeps us, as a species (and other un-interfered-with species) alive and in the food chain.

For example:

...The vast deltaic plain of the Euphrates, Tigris and Karun rivers is located at the northern end of the Persian Gulf, in extreme eastern Iraq and southwestern Iran. This alluvial basin drains a large area of Turkey, Syria, Iraq, and the western Zagros Mountains of Iran, and the basin is covered in recent (Pleistocene and Holocene) alluvial sediments. The ecoregion is a complex of shallow freshwater lakes, swamps, marshes, and seasonally inundated plains between the Tigris and Euphrates rivers. It includes huge permanent lakes of Haur al Hammar, the Central Marshes, and Haur al Hawizeh as well as more seasonal 'ahrash' forest of Populus and Tamarix on islands and banks of the great rivers. The region is among the most important wintering areas for migratory birds in Eurasia. Surveys in 1979 revealed internationally important wintering concentrations of at least 22 species (and possibly up to 70 species) of wintering waterfowl. (Source: WWF)

Hence the hunter-gatherer knows, by our innate intimacy with the solar seasonal cycle, that trapping duck was the most effective banquet-knowledge of a particularly seasonal smell or by what flowers when.

The decision of a sky 'father' or a sun 'god' was, despite the therianthropic statuary of the so-called Middle (or Near) East, that of archeologists and academics influenced completely by Abrahamic ideology. And once this dogma took hold the agreed-to decision was that these sun or sky deities were supernatural, all powerful and omnipotent. That they had anything whatsoever to anyone other than an agriculturally-bound people was dismissed.

What am I getting at? We are not separate from our landscape. We are a nutritional aspect of it and it is the stuff of our gristle and bones. The illusion of separation allows developers from far distant lands to come into a territory, talk to those that represent the illusory identity of a corporation (more like hegemonies in today's terminology) and mutually agree to the abduction and rape of a landscape for the sole purpose of profit over innovation.

Our language needs wild words. Wilderness and deep crevasse words. Words not worn frantic at being dumped on by predictability. Language that is not in a hurry. That does not need to be gr8.

Our survival (and I am including everything from bacteria and microbes to volcanic soil and voles) depends on our humanity. That we no longer ignore the genius loci's informative cloud formation and the wind god who will build to a hurricane within days. That we pay attention to the movements of ants because they do inform us of earthquakes. To the huntress arachnid mother on the window glass, guiding her millions of newborns along a single silken thread up into the eaves of the roof, informing us of the coming deluge.

Mars and Mithra are referred to as gods of war. The Roman soldiers' gods. That Mithra is a Persian representation of the sun (and what we have just considered) was adopted by the legionaries as Rome took, firstly Jerusalem, and then diverted the old Silk Road away from Nabataea, for the purposes of the financial control of the trade route, bringing knowledge of the dogma back to the capital is certain. But what they brought back to Rome was not only a sun deity. They brought back a slayer of bulls and a feaster with the sun (as a deity). What was it about this iconic idea of Mithra, that so attracted the soldiery? Was it that Greece, ever the philosophic and political entity that Rome sought to be, had been thrashed by a tyrant named Cyrus (called The Great) between 499 and 449 BCE and to an extent Rome wanted to toady to whatever powers Persia drew upon for their ferocity? I have read that Rome was highly superstitious and who wouldn't want to hang out with the victor deity? No. It united a tribe of men, until now affected by the polytheism of their fathers, under one supreme and exotic being. The cult of Mithra went underground. It became a mystery cult. An initiatory cult. Mithra, the bull-slayer, *Sol Invictus*. And these secret initiatory cults became the norm probably both inside and outside christianity. A cult of men, Mithraism shared similarities with early christianity such as liberator-savior, hierarchy of adepts—bishops, presbyters, deacons—communal meals and the dualisms of good versus evil, invented within the cult of zoroastrianism, the forerunner of everything dysfunctional in the human psyche of today.

When the horse decided we were now part of their herd, the arts of war increased exponentially. Just like Oppenheimer's involvement in science. The symbolism of a baby (actually *god-sun*) being born to a virgin in a stable covered up the idea that the wild herd-mother bequeathed us the colt that became the Trojan Horse.

Are you bored yet? I certainly am. Of this discussion of long-ago patriarchy. Of words, removed and replaced, in the 2007 Oxford Junior Dictionary.

"A" should be for acorn, "B" for buttercup and "C" for conker, not attachment, blog and chatroom, according to a group of authors including Margaret Atwood and Andrew Motion who are "profoundly alarmed" about the loss of a slew of words associated with the natural world from the Oxford Junior Dictionary, and their replacement with words "associated with the increasingly interior, solitary childhoods of today".

The religious cults and deifications that we know of today. They were not monotheistic. They were not even polytheistic. They were not theist at all. That is the opinion of a people already trapped by the hypnotic repetition of dogma. The beating down and the alienation of non-participation. Already Sleeping Beauty. What does religion do that animism cannot? Nothing. It is simply the overarching oligarchy that has gained its hold through fear and torture. And by the single idea that a somehow special man died for us. Be warned, though, of apocrypha. The doctrines of Abrahamic faiths maintain there is an end time. There will be an *armageddon*. Some of the more fundamentalist of these intertwined dogmas seek, through a terrible earth-afire ideology, just that.

Well we must counter the spell with our own. Words that take us to the fire in the meadow. Acorn, adder, ash, beech, bluebell, buttercup, catkin, conker, cowslip, cygnet, dandelion, fern, hazel, heather, heron, ivy, kingfisher, lark, mistletoe, nectar, newt, otter, pasture and willow.

The etymology, the origins, the counter-education of the conquered. Less. Commitment to not only our own health through denial of the consumerist modality—a new and virulent eco-disease—and acceptance that many so-called weeds are food. That we learn to forage and discover where our food comes from. To say less, take less, use less, be less, let go, and protect that which takes time to recover.

We can all be solutions. Healers. Wizards. All that is required, when you let slip an *Oh My God!*, is that you recognize that you said it, hear it in others, agree to an alternative, know that nothing 'out there' is going to save us from a grim, grim outcome and challenge, utterly, what we are told we are supposed to believe and to have the courage to know we know pretty much nothing. Gods are everywhere. But none of them are yours. We are relatives and, as such, should behave ourselves when a flood god or a drought god comes to our neighborhood. We should be ready, as our ancestors knew to be ready. But things are in the way, aren't they?

CONCLUSION

From INITIATION, A MEMOIR

"When I die, my body will be food for the future and so, I know I am immortal. I also know that to consider anything inanimate is not only unscientific but arrogant and crude. I don't know how slowly communities of lichen covered stone move, but I do know they move. We have always known that place contains spirit. That certain trees—a thousand years old—have knowledge of the seasons of our lives far greater than any history book. That ravens have a language we don't understand unless we listen without human ears. Most of what is read in books is the repetition of something written before, or mimics religion and carries morality.

Some people have hung with me through drought and flood and grass fire. We have walked deserts and wandered countries of heather and shaded beneath paperbark. Dug up the gravel and composted the forsaken soil. Planted forests of food and thought. We are mourning for a language not littered with objects and any need other than to be ourselves. To live our way. Color and gold, bright streams. Mists and fog hiding druids and their spells. War and confusion. The symbiosis of flesh and iron. Warrior and owl, hound and horse and boar. Blood in the water.

I won't second-guess what unfolds next. That's what this has taught me. There is now, however, a seemingly endless winding, weaving passage grave to explore, the path trod by the feet of the ancients. Those still within us. Fortresses of carved stone beneath the roots of the trees of long-dead forests. The treasure of the owl mask and the cloak of raven feathers worn upon that isle while the world was still safe, where that oak and that ash tree will thrive for a thousand years, their children dotting an eventually pristine landscape. The wilding of words and the stories that I will learn so that I can be their messenger when I am stardust.

I am the Bone Woman that reminds dogs of the snowline
That gathers the long dead and forges a terrible beauty
The mote in that bright shard of light that once was a forest
That forms the tundra
Upon which the future aurochs thunder."

14

THE HISTORY OF SNOW

LORE

NIGHT. DUSTED CLEAN WITH STARS. THE BLACK YURTS of a nomadic tribe. Fires. Family groups. Goat-like herds in a shelter of thorns. The sorceress dwelling is apart from the main group. It is only fitting. Her name is Memé and her granddaughter, Digital, is curled in her lap to listen. It'll be her turn to retell this story, word for word, when she takes initiation, becomes the next bloodline knowledge holder.

Memé, can you tell me about Snow, asks Sentence, bending to hand the old woman her tea.

Sit, Memé says, poking up the fire and sipping the brew.

Digital folds her ornately beaded chamois cloak under herself and sits in the dirt, excited.

See now, Memé begins, Snow is the Prophet and she comes from one time, then another, then another. Same world but different whenever she done the loop.

She was made by the king of the underworld. Called himself her daddy. Billy-I-Fukn-Can-Man-Silverman. Rogue-genome/recombinant DNA technician and trader. You knows what a genome is, Sentence?

We learned about it in little school, Memé.

Good. Well, species didn't get names in those days, unless humans made them up, thus King Billy-I-Fukn-Can-Man-Silverman only ever numbered Snow 327 when her cells started in on being alive. Her genetic soup was spliced together from a mixture of an Einstein gene and Billy's newest batch of survival-ready, two-legged homo-erectus animal, modified from a load of other species recombinant DNA, mainly canids like coyote and dingo and les loups and dogs and such. King Billy liked dogs.

He bought the stuff on the black market. That's the underworld. Pirates worked their trade there. Illegal stuff and exotic species, such as Snow, was sold for millions of credits.

What's a credit, Memé?

Like food only you couldn't eat it.

What were they for then?

You sure ask a lot of questions, child.

Sorry, Memé.

Anyways, I dunno, so can I keep talking?

Yes, Memé.

So, Billy was a rich man.

Memé, what's rich?

He had important stuff.

Oh, okay.

Kept a gorilla to be mummy to his breeds. And before you ask me, they was big hairy people that don't exist no more cause everything got homo-normed, okay?

Okay. Memé, but what's homo-normed?

That's people and what feeds and clothes them, and what feeds them. Nothing else was important.

That's sad.

Mm-hmm, sighed Digital from the warmth of the lap.

He'd fill that poor gorilla's womb with his DNA shots and she give birth year after year to a long line of mutations. So, we remember her and love her cause she bore Snow.

They were quiet for a minute out of respect, and Memé sipped her tea.

That gorilla mothered every species King Billy made till they was sold. He could have been rich except he was an addict.

What's an addict, Memé?

Like them lost city gals what sniffs chrome and teases menfolk that ain't too bright.

Oh, okay.

For two things. Billy loved big juicy lines of cocaine and he also couldn't resist expensive shots of exotic DNA like what made Snow.

King Billy was real impressed with Snow. He thought she was going to make him the richest man ever. She was the fastest learner of all the species he ever made. She sucked up knowledge so quick she kept him on the run for info, legal and black market, more than he really wanted to. Some might once have even thought to say he was a good Da. Snow had thought about that for just a second afore she tore out his jugular.

Cause a quick kill's a good kill, piped up Sentence, knowing it from the hunters.

She'd packed what she knew she'd need, took the gorilla by the hand and high-tailed it, sneaking and sleuthing, out of the city despite more high-tech, private-sector security patrols than you could imagine. You learned all about that in class?

Yes, Memé.

So, the two lopes for three nights through the dry, dusty, crumbling wasteland that was the dead city. Out into the badlands. Snow eated well but the gorilla died on night four because there weren't no vegetation outside no more. Least not in the low country.

Snow was so, so sad that she cried for the first and only ever time. Then she buried her mummy under a pile of rubble, so scavengers don't get to her. A sign of respect she read about sometime. Then she kept going.

Despite everything, she was wore out by the time she made it into the mountains.

Not the wastelands?

The mountains was out back of the wastelands, good girl you for picking that up, and that's where she was found by a bloke who was a tracker with one of the nests of runaways what had been rumored about. Called Illegals and made out to be the boogie man 'cause they should have been under control.

Snow's group ambushed corporation soldiers what found and exterminated Illegals and mini-nuking their nests.

The tracker bullet entered Snow's head just as the Lorentzian wormhole transported her to the exact same place, at another time or another reality, under the McCormick Bridge towpath in Chicago, Illinois in the then United States of America. It was just wide enough for junkies to hang out and shoot up and for homeless people to lie down for the night in the safety of each other's company amidst stacks of cardboard.

Snow lay unconscious and naked, in that deep, frosty night, in a pool of coagulating blood, her body temperature dropping rapidly.

Two homeless men pushed their shopping trolleys full of bulging black garbage bags, towards the underpass. The mountainous old guy, with the dirty ginger dreads tied up with lots of multi-colored twine and wearing as much clothing as one man possibly could, abandoned his mobile home when he saw Snow. He ran to her, squatting, compassionate, realizing she was still alive. He dragged off his outermost coat, covered her and tucked it all around her, dropping his ponderous self down beside her. He applied pressure to the wound to stop the bleeding and there was something about the precision of the movement that made his buddy scowl.

Ginger's done this before, thought Stone, comprehended, then, that he knew nothing of his traveling companion's life before the goon. He stood with a hand frozen to the handlebar of his trolley, unnerved and shaking with fear while chewing on a foul and talon-like pinky nail that once served to transport his drug of choice to what was left of his nose, which is what had landed him in this world of no hope in the end.

Don't do it, man. We gotta get outa here.

Not gonna happen, spat Ginger. Go get help.

Stone didn't though. He fidgeted and shuffled and pulled a fluffy ball of tissues from his pocket that he'd obviously been saving for something special because it was all still white and unused. He separated them up and begun to shred them, one by one, in abject nervousness, letting the thin, white ribbons flutter to the concrete all dead and flaccid, all the while staring at the bleeding woman.

Hurry, begged Ginger.

Stone ambled off, still shredding but also now mumbling, while Ginger pillowed Snow's head on his thigh. Even though her blood was all over him he didn't care. She just looked so helpless that he was instinctively protective, reminded of whom he'd been and of the daughter he'd lost.

. . .

The area was floodlit and cordoned off. The blue and white ribbon of crime scene tape flapped wet and flaccidly in some places, strung tight as a facelift gone wrong in others. Patrol cars bordered the cordon in a sea of flashing party lights and the city's uniformed finest held their mouths to their radios whispering secrets.

Forensics investigators in white coveralls and white gloves, albino praying mantises, were all over the scene of the seeming crime while the cops kept out of their way investigating dumpsters and shadows. Paramedics pushed and guided a gurney with Snow, laid flat and neat beneath its thermal blanket, her head swathed in bandages and a drip attached to her arm. Tucked the lot into an ambulance.

Homicide detectives Frank Spirelli and his offsider Jack Riley drove onto the scene, their siren screaming in blue revolutions. Both men pulled on disposable gloves and walked towards the interviewing cop, passing the gurney on its way to the ambulance. And that's when Frank first saw Snow.

He watched, enchanted, until the door was slammed, the siren whallow-whallowing as the vehicle left the scene. Riley scuffed his boots on the concrete until Spirelli had pulled reluctant eyes back to reality. The interviewing cop ambled over leaving his partner to annoy the old guys.

She been shot? asked Frank.

In the head. We got nothing else yet.

Snow was on the other side of a one-way mirror in a brightly-lit observation room, sitting cross-legged on the floor seemingly doing nothing. The side of her head where the hair had been shaved had a bright brown and yellow Betadine'd wound, stapled with temporary stitches.

Frank observed her from his side of the mirror.

Riley, I gotta tell you, I took one look at that broad when they were putting her in the ambulance and I'm in love.

Yeah, well, agreed Riley, I can see how that could happen, boss.

Nothing in Missing Persons. Nothing anywhere.

What's with the name Snow then?

Frank slapped the back of Riley's head.

What? Riley's offended, but then he looks back to the pale woman, his eyelids twitching. Yeah, well...

There's a bullet lodged in her brain, said Frank. Doc explained trying to remove it right now would be tempting fate.

He stared at Snow, every part of him thinking.

I mean, Riley, look at her. How does one a) live through getting shot in the head like that and b) have almost every bodily function work?

What doesn't work, boss?

She hasn't said anything. And c) be so calm.

He thought about this, calculating. Now there's pause for thought. Could calm be a symptom?

Snow listened, trying to work out the language, her lips moving ever so slightly.

Did she do it to herself, mused Riley.

Impossible. Angle of entry's all wrong. No weapon.

Riley's eyes widen with sudden understanding.

It was a hit?

It was most assuredly a hit.

X ray reckons it's made of some kind of silver compound. Kelly hasn't worked out just exactly what it is.

Well she's pale enough so maybe she's a vampire. Only she can't be, can she? I mean she's still alive.

We in some kinda B-Grade movie, Riley?

Sorry, boss.

You're an idiot sometimes, you know that don't you Riley?

Snow mouthed: *You know that don't you Riley.*

Did you see that, boss? Her bloody lips moved.

Snow wiped her lips and looked at her hand.

Frank sighed. *This is definitely my case.* His beeper went off and he checked it.

Finish up. I'll meet you downstairs.

. . .

Snow lay in bed. The nurse brought dinner, took vitals and left. Snow flicked the remote from news channel to news channel, saddened that humanity was as cacophonous and catastrophic here as where she'd come from.

She turned off the TV, took the dinner knife from the tray and padded barefoot to the bathroom.

At the sink with the mirror above it she stared at herself. Unhooked the staples, exposing the gaping wound. Calibrating, she dug into her head, feeling for the bullet. The knife maneuvered delicately through the soft tissue, but she knew what she was doing, and her brain matter, neurons and synapses moved aside like courtiers in the company of a queen. Within minutes the bullet tinkled into the sink. She washed it, staunched the wound until the blood coagulated, slid back into bed and buried the tracker in the mashed potato.

At the same time Frank drove back across town determined to stay by her side until he was sure she was safe.

. . .

The tall, pale-faced woman wore fur from neck to toe, the grizzled man beside her clad likewise. Her head was shaved on either side of its crown, an ancient scar marking the bullet's long-healed entry point. It was dissected by white tattoos, their meaning marking her as a chieftain. The remainder of her hair stood in an arching, elaborate tail bedecked with white bird of paradise feathers, while that of her companion was interwoven with those of blackbirds and crows, their quills dyed red and almost seeming a part of him. A bow was slung across her back, a quiver of arrows at either hip.

She wore the calm of one who knew secrets.

The tundra stretched endlessly in the post ice-age spring. The horses, eight hands high or more, stamped their hooves on the lichen colored rock, red as blood, and as gold as that of every armband on every man, woman and child mounted and readied for the hunt.

The wind blew towards the thousand-strong herd of aurochs that grazed upon the new spring grasses.

Snow? the man whispered.

What?

I have a question...

Not now.

Oh, okay.

Good luck, Frank.

Her stallion moved slowly forward with the silence of the elder horses, as much hunters as the people, as Frank tightened the jesses that held his spears.

15

REWILDING CHRISTMAS
(SOUTHERN HEMISPHERE EUROPEANS)

CONTEMPLATION

I'VE FIGURED OUT THE MESS THAT IS christmas, because unless you're a practicing christian why would you do it? It's because the people who added the religion to the season knew how to pitch. They have confused you.

People in the southern hemisphere need a reminder of European roots within the blood and sinew, that are deeply, if not consciously, remembered. It's an ancestral problem. Most have merely forgotten. The Celts, the Saxons, the Norse, the Normans, the Lombardian and Tuscan, the Scythians, and so many others within you, remembers. That the pine and fir are perennial, of all the European trees. You did not cut it down in the long dark. You decorated it with holly. You honored the oak king. And the mistletoe.

You have already rendered down the last of the stag fat, and your cattle are now indoors until Imbolg. You have already made the candles that will illuminate your houses through the potential season of death. One in each village window to light the shadows. A fire in the snow. Music, feasting. Wearing finely tanned fur and gold and amber talismans. With family and friends. Probably from every village in a hundred miles. Atop that hillside. It's our culture; our heritage. And we love sharing it with other cultures, which is very cool.

And I also understand the roast goose, on a 33 degree Celsius day, in Australia (won't say turkey, that's way too culturally messy). I get it. If the consumerist model, all that wasted wrapping and anything at all plastic, were removed from the equation I'd REALLY get it. I would even decorate a tree unless it was cut down vicariously and not used for fuel for the remainder of the dark days. Santa? That just creeps me out beyond anything acceptable when you think about it. Who would allow an old obese man, a stranger, into their children's bedroom unsupervised in the middle of the night?

But, you know what, witch? When will the truth override the bullshit? When will our culture of weird say no more to fitting what is expected of us by those who are not as we are? Who consider us play acting. There'll come a time, if you don't, some god or another gonna ask you to choose.

16

AN OLD STONE HOUSE
WITH THE WARPED SLATE ROOF

PORAJMOS, 1942

MY DEAR FRIEND, THIS WINTER I CAME home. The old stone house with the warped slate roof. You know it. The shutters once blue. My mother's washing, back then, horizontal in the northerly, in defiance of the ice still in the shadows. My father's sleeves above his elbows bloody with butchered goat.

The patrin nailed to our gate told the gypsies that it was safe to camp in our field. It had been there all my life. They took it down when they arrived yesterday.

Yollo's tribe has been coming since I was sixteen. Camping in the meadow beside the river. Every year. Sixty or seventy of them. On their way to the spring horse fair. They'd ride their wagons, their vardos, into a circle and liberate the big horses from the traces. The lads, half naked, rode them into the river. Like centaurs. With the dogs.
Lurchers meant to hunt the forests of the gentry.

They'd invited us to eat at their fire. To come at deep twilight. Mother had said no.

Gadji, Baldo whispered to the man beside him. An insult, I was to learn.

Father always ignored her. Stayed up late drinking with them. Playing music and admiring the women dancing. He had his own father's accordion in those days. With the ivory keys and the mother of pearl bass buttons. Mother kept me inside at night, for as long as they stayed. The people in her village had shunned them when she was a girl. Would not allow them to camp in the field by their river. Had told her they were thieves. The men would rape her. Had been told never to trust them.

Hypocrite, I'd thought. I always saw her. Always in the indigo dark of the third night after they arrived. That wagon at the edge of everything. To Boboko, the drabarni who read her fortune in her cards.

Mother came home haunted the last time. All those years ago. I'd felt it too, although I could not have articulated the dread.

Yollo was two years old when they first came. I remember his widowed father Baldo, the Rom baro, lifting him onto the massive pied horse with the shaggy-haired feet. I was besotted. Baldo was twice my age but with hooded black eyes that danced all over me and who smiled when I did, when my mother wasn't watching. He made my groin ache. I was ripe enough to marry but to him? That was fantasy. Of course.

The following year I was accepted into the university to study art. Mother and Father both died in the winter. Long story. I'll tell you about it if I ever see you again.

Only two dozen or so came yesterday. Eyebrows etched with hoarfrost, scarves covering their mouths, so I could not tell who I knew. Guiding the wagons through the white air, into the meadow beside the river. No smoke from the chimneys. The old men walking. Uncoupling the horses. Hobbling them. Leaving them to find the elusive young tips of spring grass. New mothers on back steps, breastfeeding. Boboko's vardo no longer with them. No young men other than Yollo. And him the Rom baro now. Big man at twenty. Rings on all his fingers. I haven't asked what happened to the others and he hasn't said.

I'm glad they're here. I don't mind at all. I intend to line my boots with the feathers from the dozen pigeons cooking in the pot over the coals in the courtyard. God, those men can use a slingshot like my father could a gun.

My friend, when you visit your wife in Powązki, and you pass by Piotre's grave, my husband's grave, will you hum beneath your breath for me that I love him still? Will you let him know that I am happy today? I am glad he died so gently and so young. Unlike his brothers. Unlike my family.

Oh, that's right. I almost forgot and it's amazing. The walnut wood clock on the mantle works again. Yollo's sister, the current *drabarni* with the peroxide-blonde hair and the crow eyes, glanced at it on her way outside. Raised her eyebrows at its petulance. It hesitated. Then the pendulum swung as smooth as slipper satin. After so many years. Fancy that.

Warsaw is gone. My university. But I will not think these thoughts tonight.

A foxful of magic. A horse fair in the tenderness of spring. They ask if they might stay till then. I ask that they please do. And will you play music here? And may I dance? Yollo grins at me. His front teeth are gold.

He is not to lose them until the Nazis find us.

17

INTERVIEW WITH AMERICA

A CONVERSATION BETWEEN **LY DE ANGELES**, AUSTRALIA AND **DANETTE WILSON** (AND KALLAN KENNEDY) AMERICA

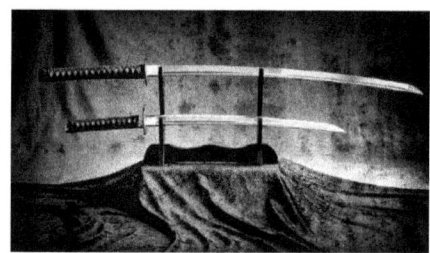

DANETTE: THANK YOU SO VERY MUCH Ly for letting us ask you a few questions. I shared with Kallan Kennedy, my editor, for the Sunday Stew, and she has a couple questions for you as well.

Q: On your website you write, "I wish to acknowledge the Wurundjeri People of the Kulin Nation in whose country I now live." So, my first question is if you can tell me more about these people and share some experience of time you may have spent with them? How have they enhanced your magic?

A: I acknowledge the First Nation People because it is the honourable thing to do. We should all be utterly offended by the rape and decimation of indigenous nations. It has always been done, I know. Although my studies of such only go back to Rome's invasions of Europe and Britain (the Norse did so previously but never to the same extent) all of Europe,

Africa, Canada, USA, Polynesia, South America, New Zealand, Australia. Bullets and beads. Oh, and then the christian missionaries set about destroying ways as ancient and sustainable as time.

I had no contact with indigenous people until I moved to Byron Bay in the north back in 1991. I have potent contacts up that way, with both Kadaicha and Featherfoot of more than one country, all with their stories of tragedy.

It happened to my ancestors, over and over again, and yet, until I recently wrote *Priteni* the telling of that story has always been an oral thing. David, long-time friend, once lover, is the son of an indigenous woman (I do not have permission to say more) but his father was a Scotsman, and a brutal drunk. He was ashamed of his "white blood".

"You give us a wasteland and call it peace," I quoted to him. "What?" he asked. I repeated the quote. "Who said that?" "Calgacus. Your ancestor," I replied, "before the battle against Rome." He watched me for a while without responding. Considering I don't know what. Then he said, "Did we win?"

Currently the Australian constitution does not recognise the First Nations as even existing and it is only a few years since the term *terra nullius* was abolished thanks to Eddie Mabo. Acknowledgement before any event, within any work, is both an emotional and a political statement by a strong movement for a parliamentary voice. There are many *countries* in what the invaders call Australia, and they are all different. Same in USA? Are the First Nations acknowledged thus there? No. I know. I've checked. It took a lot of bloodshed in Ireland for the language to be revived, for the landscape to be named in the language of the indigenous people. Same in Wales. We've a long way to go. There's been so much harm done.

I have shared the stories of the subjugated Celtic tribes with indigenous people here in Australia. Because almost nobody knows about us no one told them, ever. Did you learn about Boudica in school? No. Were you taught about *The Pale*? Most with whom I have spoken just thought us pompous, self-righteous invaders, taking from them their identities and replacing them with christianity, chains or death, stealing them from their families and giving them English names.

Q: *Priteni* sounded so wonderful I went to Amazon and ordered it right off. My father's family is from Scotland and Ireland and I have embraced my Celtic roots, but your thirty years of research is certainly my next question. What has kept you inspired and amazed for such a long time?

A: I don't like delusion. If there's a true story to be found, rather than what we hope or want, I'll hunt it down if I can.

Now... As for that (and here I go offending an entire raft of people, yet again) the same applies to that which I revere. Dion Fortune, and so many who have written after her (including me, so I will clear all this up here) said, "All gods are one god, all goddesses are one goddess and there is but one initiator." What's that? Fortune, Gerald Gardner, Alex Sanders, and so very many that have written since, have postulated just this. And it incorporates, merges and morphs very, very diverse cultural and ethnic spiritualities and mysteries into a hodgepodge amalgamation of anthropomorphic deities. It is just plain incorrect. Witchcraft Theory and Practice. That's 101. When we truly grow up we should ask, *are we trading one form of religion for another.* The answer is yes.

Even before I came to awareness of the above over the last twelve years, I had that rough-around-the-edges feeling that there was more to witchcraft than the rehashing words and reading material that others, of a relatively modern society, and a predominantly christian one at that, have presented. Of deity names ad hoc and ad nauseum. Without deep scholarship or deeper contemplation. Yeats once wrote "Naming is treacherous because naming divides truths into half-truths making them a coffin of counters. Be careful. Give the spell no name."

Hunting for the history stories, myths and legends of Europe and Ireland, England before it became England, France when the tribe dwelling in what is now known as Paris is the Parisi, the Belgae to the north, the Caledon in what is now Scotland. Finding the lore of the Firbolg, knowing that the Dumnon (the people of contemporary Cornwall) provided the tin for the Bronze Age that went as far as China along the Old Silk Road. All spoken of as though dead and gone. All recounted in the past tense as though we are extinct.

Do witches need to know this? Of course. What's the point of studying that which is fabricated? What have I unearthed, though, when it comes to meeting and truly communing with this landscape, or that star patter, or the wall at the back of the garden that still remembers the river, that others call *god* and *oddess*, as though there is only two genders, and as though the god of thunderclap or kookaburra is listening? They are now rock and headland, river and sparrow—One of my ancestors is the country of the tribe called Brigantians (present-day Lancashire/Yorkshire). And it is written that their *deity* is female and is called Brigid. And isn't that strange? Why? Is 'she' the same as in Ireland? The answer is no. Brigid, named for the tribe, is the god Pennines. The word *brigid* is roughly 'high one' and are, therefore, genius loci. We Pennines are mountains, rivers, wells, shelter; boar and stag and bear and every healing plant and every necessary poison and visionary mushroom. Interwoven. Summer following spring. Trees communicating through colour and sap, root and underground fungal systems and networks. Salmon and wolves, bears and golden hunting eagles, hare and hounds. That's it. You see it? Pipers and drummers. There yet?

When people lump it all together, invoke the feminized deities Kali and Isis, or say that Asherah and Diana are the same, what is removed from our language is the uniqueness, not only of the people of the region where these gods and they, intertwine, but the knowledge they must share with us, who are *not* them. What we have are stories, and stories keep us curious. Take something for granted and we become complacent. Certain mushrooms will kill our kids.

When we live with the delusion of separation how can magic really work? Without the consensual agreement of the whole that is the sovereign space of existence?

Even here in Melbourne, and remember this is not my ancestral

anything, I know that if I travel ten suburbs from my home I am in another country. One can feel these secret, unseen borderlands. Who sets them? No one. They simply are. Ravens know their territory. They call it at sunset from four directions. They are leys, dragon-lines. I know I need to get onto your next question but if I may conclude by including aspects of your first question regarding the Wurundjeri, or the Bundjalung, or the Dja Dja Wurrung people, or the Ojibwa, Navaho, Comanche, Maori, Brigantach, Tuatha Dé Danann, Scythian people, Samé… I could go on… is that we know, because we have been earth, since before earth became earth. I realise that's an assumption because even now the theory of the Big Bang is being torn to shreds but, because nothing comes from nothing, we have, in our DNA, the knowledge of eternity. That each person is 90% bacteria and 10% human should inform us of our insolence at considering ourselves superior to anything! We should not be slack and accept only what modern texts tell us about anything, let alone what it is to be witch.

If it has the taint of religion about it, it is suspect.

Q: You say that "one of the heroes is a great, great grandfather." Could I enquire one awesome resource and some advice for our readers and myself you might share on researching your family lineage and roots?

A: My colleague, of over thirty years, Bernard Casimir, is a renowned genealogist. His work is painstaking, but he's been at it for forty years. All genealogical work is thus because it (again) is so easy to make shit up for the sake of an identity. He's hunting through parish registers from four hundred years ago, translating wills and notaries from the 12th century. Back through what are called Rolls and Titles. Following riverbeds that never disappear from the landscape. Sure, they can be rerouted by such things as the Great Famine, the Black Plague, the

Holocaust, but tributaries exist that can become major rivers into the depths of who you are. Language has changed, letters are almost unrecognisable. It's quite a craft. I'm an adopted person and I began the quest (originally) for my actual time of birth so I could get an accurate astrological chart. Over years more and more information became available through post-adoption resources. I obtained documents from my maternal line and Bernard was able to trace four distinct lineages. All that is required to begin the process is the birth/death certificates of one's biological parent/s and their parents.

What happens, because of unearthing all these people, is the surety of a vastly deep history. It changed me. To know one's identity from five hundred years ago, two thousand? Realizing just how many people are of the same ancestry. It's like awakening all these people in one's own veins. Death loses any power over us.

Q: You mention, in your bio, of two near-death experiences (drowning and electrocution). Can you elaborate? I know there is a story to this.

A: No, not really. Not about them per se. I was eleven. It was an astonishing year. Everything that could possibly have happened that year did happen (including my first taste of renown). It was like a 'quickening' psychically, emotionally and with my writing. I've since almost died countless times in this one body. It's almost hilarious that I'm still here.

Q: I loved reading about your getting lost in nature as a kid, being a book addict and your wonderful grandmother. What is your best memory of your grandmother or time spent with her?

A: When I first met her? The smell of her. She smelled of violets. As well as reading cards and tealeaves she managed the Rembrandt Hotel in Kings Cross. That hotel also smelled exotic. Of old sandstone and deep, cool outdoor gardens. The hallways smelled of the pleasures experienced in them and, also, behind closed doors, in those pre-sixties years. The jazz and blues musicians on R & R during the Second World War stayed there. What an exquisite art deco experience. Ceramic naked women supporting globe lights along art-hung hallways, the old gaslights still on the walls, concertina elevator doors of polished brass with a boy on a stool wearing a little red hat working the levers. The smells of her hotel. The sight of her in long-dead, silver fox furs. The gift of a Maori paua shell bracelet (she'd lived in New Zealand before immigrating to Sydney). Later, when she lived with us, her humour and her readings that were so accurate they were deadly. My favourite memory, however, was when she died. She'd predicted it the week before, but I just didn't understand. She'd read my teacup and said that between then and next Tuesday my mother was going to be extremely upset by events beyond her control. It wasn't the death, however. When my mother went to set up funeral arrangements and have Marion's body transferred to the funeral home, to do what they do, she was told there wasn't one. My grandmother had donated herself to science and had already been sent off to a university. My mother cremated an empty coffin.

Q: Byron Bay is gorgeous, and reminds me of Cornwall. How did you end up there, and is it magical?

A: How funny. It's nothing like Cornwall from my perspective. More like Ibiza! I lived there for twenty-two years and there's a tale of great mystery and magic to be told about the getting there, but we'd be here all day, so I won't. When my family and I relocated there in 1991 it was into the belly of magic. It was strong for almost two decades and I had a whopper of a coven, produced and directed several shows, raised my kids, worked with teens in trouble to learn the arts, and wrote several books. Consumerism is now rampant and the greedy paw over the dead flesh of honesty like maggots. Too many drugs, too many failed dreams. Too much exclusivity. Too many secret beatings, ice, pot that's had the antipsychotic cannabinoid, CBD, bred out of it. Schizophrenia. Suicide. My sons and their children are still there.

Q: Iaido, the sword skills of the Samurai warriors sounds fascinating and I want to enquire, how has your martial arts blended with or enhanced your witchcraft and magic?

A: I'm a very physical woman. Tactile. Curious. I also love weights and still work out, at a gym, three days a week. Iaido, Hapkido, Aikido and MMA. Worked them all. I learned to kill and defend, yes, but then I realised I needed more so I did a senior first aid certificate (brown snakes around Byron Bay. They'll kill you if you don't know how to bandage the limb bitten) so I knew how to set a bone or resuscitate a person in cardiac arrest. Then I joined the Regional Emergency Road Rescue Squad and drove a truck and stood with a cop, holding a blanket to keep the sight-seers from staring at the boy whose legs were crushed by a side-swipe, listening to the ambos' no-nonsensing him into hope, then taking his mother aside so they could do their job and she wouldn't have to panic. None of them stared at the tattoos on my face; the cops just said, "Thank god you're here." I figure he meant "thank life." I love the challenge of learning a new skill. That's magic, you know, among other things. Wonder.

Q: What advice do you have for someone interested in embracing Native American culture and how to approach learning from elders where we live?

A: One can't embrace it unless one is Native American. We can learn from them everything they are willing to teach but no one should push. Anglo and European people haven't earned the right. That's important. To accept responsibility. Has anyone apologized? No. Same applies to the slave trade of African Americans and that continuing injustice. I learned a while back about intergenerational trauma. We all suffer it. The disregarded and disenfranchised more than any. Thank you for asking that question.

Danette: Kallan also has a couple of questions…

Kallan: How does the indigenous view differ from that of mainstream wicca and other pagan belief systems?

A: Walking the walk is the bottom line. Everything to do with knowledge and silence. The more we talk without good reason the less the voices of those who really need to be heard will be heard. That's not just people. That's species. The white rhino. How many left? Three? The water off the coast of Rio Doce in Brazil? The hole in the ozone above me? Those sinkholes in Siberia? Fukushima? We're all facing peril. Witches. Pagans. We're beheaded in Saudi Arabia. Massacred in New Guinea, Haiti and parts of Africa. Most mock us as useless or non-existent or dress their children in black pointy hats and paint their faces green at what they call hallowe'en; Samhain—which, by the way, is the end of April in Australia—and still parents help dress their children in ghoulish garb and send them out to beg for sugar. A little creepy, don't you think, when we usually suggest they don't talk to strangers?)

We do not use our voices as indigenous people of earth. Too many still do christmas. Not enough know their own bones, or are really useful at anything. Wicca has become mainstream, yes. I am not wiccan. I respect anyone's right to believe what they do, to a degree. Respect is an earned thing. Paganism is a very generic word. Witch embraces the word heretic and anarchy (the right to choose and challenge mainstream concepts of authority).

Q: You often speak of the earth having a conversation with us. Can you expound on this a bit for our readers? What advice would you have for those who want to listen/respond, but don't know how?

A: Everybody should grow enough organic food to share with others. Know where food comes from, stop Big Corp from poisoning us with pre-packaged food by taking your cloth bag to the fish monger, the green grocer, the butcher. Ask them to wrap your goods in paper not plastic. Get rid of plastic.

Food and drug companies are in the cancer-making market. They're killing you. Stop consuming, start hunting, Be fussy. Love the life of what you eat. Find out how your meat or fish is killed. Is it antibiotic and hormone-free? Don't buy from supermarkets. Don't feed your kids junk. Get away from your mobile phones and read *Toxin Toxout* so you know where your possessions come from, what they do to you and your family, where they end up.

Learn to talk with dogs. Ride with horses. Climb things to find out if you're as strong on the outside as you are on the inside. Shame the man, or the institution, hurting the woman or the child. Have an opinion about gender and sexuality but don't judge unless it concerns non-consensual abuse. Be kind to one another. Be kind anyway. Knowledge is masterful. Knowledge is magic.

When we accept responsibility for what we even think we are, clearing silent spaces for earth to communicate. Stop considering that aliens create crop circles. Earth is talking. Oh, you won't listen? I'll blow a few volcanoes, send hurricanes of maximum force. Earth killed off all the rock stars in 2016. Showing us the incredible power of communication. If we don't listen to the weather? Be proactive in meaningful ways.

One can cast a ritual circle and make a wand from willow withies, can celebrate Llughnasad and the cycles of the moon. And cast spells. For what? You think they're going to work? They do, but do you know why? The whole point of being witch, is responsibility in the true meaning of the word. Is to hold a mirror with the glass facing out because we have looked so far within we're game enough. Being the person that children ask questions of, because they know we won't lie and if we don't know then at least we can say so. The shaman, the sorcerer.

My grandchildren know me as witch. I feed them exquisite food and stories. At midsummer and midwinter, when everyone from educators to double-base and sax players bring laughter and food to our house, the kids are embraced and included. They know christmas is a cultural lie; are freaked out at the worship of the image of a tortured, agonized dead man, kept perpetually alive in the imagination, and of his Da who supposedly set the scene. What does that say of our society?

Danette: Thank you so much for this opportunity to share.

Danette Wilson can be found at her blog, redwitchesjourney.com/

18

A MIND LIKE CLEAR WATER

AT END OF THE KUMIJO CLASS, WHERE I trained with staff and bokken, the class was seated on the mats. The fellow who had stood in for the sensei talked about the conscious and subconscious mind; that the subconscious was white and positive, and that if we had negative thoughts – black – they would go into the subconscious and turn it grey.

What a disappointing discussion.

Dualisms like good/bad, black/white, positive/negative merely reinforce the stereotypical paradigms that have become a religious and political tool—as well as a major advertising ploy—for manipulating people into an untrue view of what is acceptable or otherwise. It's seemed like it's been done forever. These concepts are just that. Concepts. They have no mirror in life.

So, what's the reality?

The dissolution of androcentric mind. The breakthrough. An absolution from thinking 'humanly' to the denial of everything else, except, perhaps, peripherally.

ANALOGY—

Not far from where I lived, in Byron Bay, is a place called Protestors Falls. At the end of a track that meanders through the rainforest is a deep pool fed from a waterfall that cascades down a two hundred and forty foot escarpment. It can be quite loud there beside the pool, sitting upon boulders that embrace it, because the place is a natural amphitheater. Bat-caves are high up in the cliff face, ferns and native plants defy gravity from rocky outcroppings. Sitting there you can look up towards the top of the falls. The experience is akin to reverse vertigo. The sky sits on top of it all in such a vivid blue as to hurt the eyes. Birds whip-call across the valley.

I've been there as dusk turns to dark and the profusion of fireflies warp the senses in the darkness as they flicker between huge trees and land on my eyelashes. The place is mythic. It fills me with awe. The water from the falls comes from elsewhere—higher up—from amongst the gorges and gullies, catchments for rain and spring-fed creeks.

From where it thunders or trickles, depending on the season, into the deep pool at its base, it murmurs and tumbles down and down, over rock and rock and rock, linking with other creeks and waterways until it reaches the sea.

Along the journey of its destiny are habitats. Frogs live there. Lizards. Birds and snakes, paddymelons, echidna, wallabies, turtles and, so I have been told, platypus. They have lived around or in the waters of this place since the Dreamtime.

But tour buses sometimes bring people here. And isn't it nice to take a dip in the deep, deep pure waters of the pool at the base of the falls? They are responsible for the decimation of these habitats; for the poisoning of these waters. They wear deodorant, perfume, sunblock, make-up, hair product; false things, toxic things. And if someone just told them to be clean of all these things first? To enter the waters aware? Would they?

The subconscious is not a void, nor is it a mess. It can be a garden or a forest of wild profusion – that depends on the *nature* of the person—it doesn't matter which. But each mind is unique and will flourish as long as it remains in its natural state. We must be very careful to prevent that which is toxic, or noxious, or alien, from gaining hold. To do this requires a modicum of detachment. From emotional detachment and detachment from the material. From buying into the jargon or the expectations of others. From outside interference that seeks to tell you what is right or wrong, black or white, positive or negative, light or dark.

A mind like clear water takes care. It requires love and it needs to be left alone sometimes. To be quiet.

Your body will usually inform you of when you are being pressured or polluted by unnatural things. It will suffer agitation or tension; your gut will express anxiety; your head will experience pressure, maybe your hands will shake. Perhaps you will suffer from 'want' and this will cause confusion and sometimes even despair. Maybe you won't sleep so well anymore. Let it go. Take it off yourself. Fix it.

I've swum in that pool at the base of Protestors Falls, naked and clean. I've straddled the god rock, in the heart of the waters.

I learned from that god, to have a mind like clear water.

(Since first writing this, I have been informed swimming in the god pool at the base of the falls has been banned because of the ecological damage being caused by tourism. Happy is this word-witch with *that* spell).

BELTANE IS NOT HALLOWEEN

On the European-Australian Celebration of Springtime

Melbourne's famous street art

THE CROSSOVER BETWEEN WINTER AND SUMMER

INTRODUCTION

I'm in Melbourne, Australia. And this season does the hoochie cooch of European trees in their green glam and fruit tree blossom that brings bees and permeate our deep veins of memory. Ancestral bones dancing at midnight as dusk slides a little less quickly into day. And my day begins at sunset. Everything is born from a dark place. It's imperative to actually use one's senses. Closest to (perihelion) and furthest from the sun (aphelion) have agreed to the dates. These are only dates in the modern sense and that's okay, but they are a construct. Dates in a diary create hook ups and a collective unity. But that's what they are. Witchery is the knowing beyond the constructs. Earth and sky inform us. Wind in epic howling moving detritus hither and thither.

Redistributing seedpod and bee roads. Even the mozzies are back.

INDIGENOUS CELTS

Céadsamhradh is Irish for the beginning of summer. It's a celebration. If one wants to create a ritual for it so be it. It's when our world wakes up, post spring and (in my case) I begin the major planting because I know there will be no surprise frosts. So, in go the tomatoes, auberges and zucchini. Feasting is the best thing. Light fires and candles, or a barbecue for a haunch of goat. People used fire to burn the winter bedding of broom or straw which would, by this time of year, be disgusting and riddled with wildlife.

TRADITIONS KNOWN AND CONCEPTUALIZED

Cattle were known to be passed between two fires. Ever the pragmatist I would suggest the smoke kills off parasites suffered through the long dark. The relatives in our blood didn't leave written records. Julius Caesar in his Commentary on the Gallic Wars (De Bello Gallico 6,16) purports that the Brits loaded animals and humans into a giant wicker structure and burned them alive. This has been disputed and called wartime propaganda. There is no evidence. But I will suggest that tribes, having survived a recent glaciations period, are not about to waste good food. And slaves were worth almost as much as cattle. Criminals, the annals say, were killed in this structure but had Julius Caesar had a conversation with Brehons and druids? No. *He* never got that close. We certainly did give gifts of people, brooches and swords to the land and the wells and the bogs. I would speculate that we did not/do not differentiate between species and art. One is certainly no more important than the other. We're all earth.

FAKE NEWS: EVENTS AS A TOOL OF PROPAGANDA

A specific killing technique called a threefold death was employed, as recognized in bodies exhumed from bogs, mummified and tanned, a kind of formal gift for, again speculation, what was probably a very good reason. But have a read of the language of the translation. If this isn't religious, abrahamic and bilious diatribe I don't know what is. It would take us an afternoon and several strong coffees to translate it into a Celtic consciousness.

Caesar, *De Bello Gallico 6.161 Sacrificial Customs of the Gauls* "The entire nation of the Gauls is very given to religious scruples, and for this reason, those who are affected by grave diseases, and who take part in battle and in peril, either sacrifice men as victims or vow to sacrifice them, 1 16. *Natio est omnis Gallorum admodum dedita religionibus, atque ob eam causam, qui sunt adfecti gravioribus morbisquique in p roeliis periculisque versantur, aut pro victimishomines immolant aut se immolaturos vovent administrisquead ea sacrificia druidibus ut untur, quod, pro vita hominis nisihominis vita reddatur, nonposse deorum immortaliumnumen placari arbitrantur, publiceque eiusd em generis habentinstituta sacrificia. Alii immani magnitudine simulacra habent, quorum contexta viminibus membra vivis homini buscomplent; quibus succensis circumventi flamma exanimanturhomines. Supplicia eorum qui in furto aut in latrocinio autaliqua n oxia sint comprehensi gratiora dis immortalibus essearbitrantur; sed, cum eius generis copia defecit, etiam adinnocentium supplicia descendunt.*

"And they use druids as the performers of these sacrifices, because they believe that, unless for the life of a man, the life of a man is returned, the power of the immortal gods is not able to be appeased, and they have instituted sacrifices of this kind for the public. Others have images great in size, the limbs of which, interwoven with twigs, they fill with living humans; the men, with these having been set aflame, perish. The punishments for those apprehended in conspiracy or in thievery or in other crime are thought to be most pleasing to the immortal gods; but, when abundance of this kind fails, they even defer to the punishment of the innocent."

I want to strip it and rip it to pieces because *there was no nation*. This was a system of highly independent tribes trading as far away as what is now China and Iceland throughout the bronze age. Speculatively, again, across the Baring Strait into the lands of the Americas and even further south. Quetzalcoatl was a redhead. The concept of "immortal gods", no! The above is propaganda.

Why we agree to accept this drivel as true I'll never understand. The deeper into my hoary era I dive the more questions I invoke than ever. Neither Julius nor those interpreting or writing about supposed events down through the bowel of the ages were anthropologists, social or otherwise. They were there to take. To pillage, cause ruin, to impose.

We know this because it is still perpetuated on indigenous people everywhere. It's a monkey see, monkey do thing. A Pavlov's dog behavior.

And the hallow'een thing being perpetuated in Australia, on October 31st? I couldn't be bothered that revelers are doing this here as spring displays grandeur without them, because it's a good excuse for them to get ghoulish. The day went from… Which is pretty funny but… It is a Celtic thing. And both the above elements have buried us. Am I offended? Absolutely. Sucked in and fueled by the capitalist consumerist model. Being conned. So. Don't think of the month. Feel. Recognize.

LOOK TO THE STARS

The calendar we are ensorcelled by is Gregorian. It is known as a western one (we must discuss this and break that term upon the back of the Greek philosophers' arrogant wheel). A christian reckoning of days, created by a papal bull issued by pope Gregory XIII in 1582. May/October. The months thus named as samhain and samhradh are irrelevant. Proponents of hallow'een do exactly what those benefitting from easter and christmas do: they mangle together the seasons of the aphelion, the descent into the long night, an ancient time of possible death, therefore a time to fear, with a 'holy day'. Halloween is, of course, hallowed (holy) eve, or the night before All Saints Day, or the feast of the solemnity of all the saints. Yet another excuse for church attendance and an opportunity to pass the tithing plate. A so-called celebration of the link between those already in the christian heaven and those of them still unwontedly earthbound. See the likeness? And why Samhain has been called the day of the dead when we invite the ancestors to dinner?

We ARE the ancestors. We are all still here. Gather those you love.

Play music. Get safely drunk. Eat succulently. Explain enough so that in a year's time you don't need to.

Image Beltane Fire Society

19

THE FIRST FOREST

THE CAIRN OF DOLMEN STONES, MOSSES and lichens covering the swirls and patterns that mark a forgotten ancestry, stands silent and brooding upon the hilltop, sentinels that guard an ancient gate that opens onto the Dreaming Lands. Half hidden amidst alder and oak, the quiver of aspen the before-time stunted spruce.

Day softens with dusk, but the signs of summer, subtle as they are, can be seen, felt and heard; the chitter of dormice in the gorse thicket, the ruffle and flurry as the night owl preens white wings.

The sun dips towards the horizon, creating mysterious depths and hollows within the rough circle of still-warm stones, as they cast their long shadows upon the ground.

This is the first world. Before the one you inhabit. When the world was born. I am a night wind—storyteller of shadows, carrier of weather, friend of hurricane and monsoon alike—and always I wake from the sleep of the light between the sunset and the dark when the world gets just a little calmer.

And always I wake, as a kiss upon the air, within this place of secrets.

At first glance the circle seems empty, its stillness unbroken, its unseen power humming softly. But then I see him move (it was not a shadow after all).

The mountainous dark man, in his big old army greatcoat, threadbare jeans and heavy lace-up boots, with dreadlocks, like the roots of trees, falling in a cascade down his back, all threaded here and there with blackbird feathers, catching the fading light in their blue-black sheen, and littered here and there with the flittering of living things, the bones of dead ones. He stands as still as the stones themselves, facing into the sunset to say farewell to yesterday. I know at once just who he is.

People call him Hunter and he is a first forest; a forest god. He is also the wolves that roam in search of dinner, Crows that pick a carcass clean, ants that take what even the crows could not see, and the webs and fungus and neural network that informs of the health of habitat. He is still alive despite how many try to cut him down, kill him off, or dredge him or dig him to death, in your time.

It's been oh, an age since he has come to this gate. A thousand years or more spent wandering the ancient trackways to remind earth of beauty, of fecundity; that he is them, and me, and the gang down in the valley, and we are all still here. I sense the first people—the fáidh—and I know they'll keep the fires burning against a night not of us—not clean—that's yet to be.

The sun's a final eye-watering blade of molten gold upon the horizon, before then vanishing abruptly, leaving a crimson and pale mauve sky to slowly darken, brushed with stars. Hunter folds his arms across his chest and begins a low, terrible, beautiful song. The words are in the old tongue – the voices of burns and howling snowstorms –meant to evoke yearning in the memories of those who think themselves forgotten.

Darkness now hastens to claim its center of the ring, and as the last of the light forgets itself Hunter turns to face inwards, into the company of ragged stones, bringing the calling to a close.

I can't read his thoughts, but I understand the sad and haunted light behind his black, steady gaze. It's fortunate indeed that I am here now for I can blow the cobwebs of doubt away.

He is still for a moment only, then he moves to close a circle within the circle of stones, shutting out the other world.

Night wakes the badger and the white-faced storm petrel, the spectacled bear and the civet. They leave the safety of daytime dens and burrows and begin the relentless search for prey to feed their young, and I swirl about them, also, sending downwind scents of that which decays and that which yet lives, in equal measure.

I also sense him. Loss, and a relentless determination in the face of so much tragedy, that both dwell behind the iron-strong discipline.

Hunter is draíocht, you see. The fire of inspiration. All the legends and the patterns and the spells – the whole of him. And he knows that I am here, but I'm not the one he seeks.

A fat and buttery moon is rising now, splashing amber on the fallen long-stone on which he sits to wait, causing shadows to deepen even more. A familiar scene becomes ethereal, filled with older mysteries.

This is the time between.

This is the time, in ages past, when he would normally leave, abandoning us to the dark, to travel in the world that you now know, in the company of the sídhe, those immortal people waiting down in the valley, join them in searching for the lost, or the hated, in your time, their fate determined by the doing that they'll do.

He sits on that great fallen stone and I hear his breathing as it comes a little faster, just a little harder, as the presences other than both of us arrive - guardians of the stones and whisperers of ancient magic older still than any of us.

There. Within the deep shadows of the furthest dolmen arch, a small figure, clothed, it would seem, from the swirling night itself; a darkening and a thickening of the shadows, and as black as the deepest, skyless cave.

Walking into the ring on two legs, wearing a cloak of night, it appears in a woman's form.

In his customary quiet voice, he asks 'Are you all of us, then?'

The god wearing the woman-body and face smiles and moves, and from within the dark folds of that cloak tiny, brilliant points of light shine and glitter like stars, mirroring the current sky. Then mists roil and swirl like forgotten ghosts, and a murder of ravens, swoops from the depths with a rattle of wings and a hundred conversations, to fly, mad and carefree, to places in your world – messengers, oracles – to those who still know how to recognize the signs.

'You know me, Hunter?' The voice soft and deep.

'I think so. Are you—?'

'The hidden depths of anything? Yup, that's me Hunter. Silence, and patience, and stillness. The burgeoning womb and the peaceful tomb, when they're each other anyway. The bare bones of all that is, and the time it takes to crumble them to dust, and the earth to claim them for the garden.

'Oh, and I'm the visions that the dreamer seeks. You know how this Amergin-thing goes, Hunter. You okay? You look a little bleak.'

'I'm okay,' sighs Hunter.

The cruelties and violence, the apathies he's witnessed are laid bare for this over-arching god, wearing a woman's body, to know. No other could look and not be frightened for the future. This god is earth's memory-keeper.

'It's not over yet,' she whispers gaily.

'I'm tired,' says Hunter, finally able to relax the burden of keeping wonder alive within the tangle of tomorrow.

'Shove over…' He does, and she sits beside him, tucking young, gangly legs beneath her, like a child, 'so I can breathe the forest that I smell on you.

He's smiling now.

'Love, Hunter. You know about love?'

'Yeah, I know about that.'

I fly up, and reach out, and carry back the distant sound, first of Matt's piping, then Willie the Red's fiddle, then Alan's bodhràn.

My attention strays, for not even a second, and he's alone. He stands and shakes his coat out like big khaki wings, starlight falling from it to the ground.

I HAVE TOUCHED YOU

ON LOVE AND THE WILD GOD

I have touched you with the hands of many ages and
Have wrapped around you poems, from a forest deep and ancient.
I have loved you clean of rage, enough I hope, for you to know it
As the rage towards those who'd bring you down upon their hunt to dour day, the stag within you, wild, enchanted, lost on concrete streets that know no giving.

Oh, child, you are a creature from some legend, and behind your sight hang veils in temple doorways

And I know how long it's haunted you through all the times you challenged trust, to find it only endless dust.

The choices all are lying in some secret grove where passion calls them. Flowers in the moon-wind. Pick them, oh, so gently for their beauty fades when they are known too long. Like a spell too early spoken, like a dream too long forsaken.

I see you in the forest deep, wild rose and mosses at your feet
And mists, like ghosts, between huge trees; I see you gently bend your knees and kiss the earth with lips and tears.

The memory of such as you, who can slay or save because, despite,
Whose shadowed eyes confound, delight,
Who bows the head to none in shame.

Will give life, this woman who was wildling-born,
The raven and the rose's thorns, good reasons for continued dawns.

So. With candles lit within the night the ritual summons sanity. I remember love. I remember you. The hunter, spirit of pride, clan's destiny. Not the killer, the coward, the pretender, the grief of the office-worker's plight.

If we are not careful we lose.

AUTHOR'S NOTE

WITCHES, YES YOU, BECAUSE YOU ARE still with me. Either that or you like to see the last pages first. So...

WELCOME TO MY TABLE.

Sit. Put your feet up. Let's chat about something important....

Before we have books, we are cultures of art and story, weavers, singers, makers of magic to call the herd, to summon the bear. We are the architects of Stonehenge and, with antler bone, diggers of thirty-foot-deep chalk ditches. For the acoustics, for the singers and the musicians. We decorate our hair with the thin bones of our mother's and father's winter whale hunt, that massive old elk who gave herself up for the  kill, to protect the young. We craft jet or turquoise into beads to decorate our boots of soft leather. Carve jade into figurines. We waste nothing because tomorrow might bring the return of the Howler, spoken of softly, venerably, to appease this ancestor into passivity.

Into leaving our elders and children alive. How did we learn what was edible and what would kill us? That this mushroom is for supper and this, for initiation; for the visions? All of us, before the advent of books, tell each other stories, remind ourselves of ancient wisdom through chant and repetition. We dance the memories of direction and wellsprings, the building of boats and the reading of starlight to guide us across the sea.

Story is how. Word of mouth. It still works even though not all of it is true. Some stories seek to drag us into religious cults. Careful of them, puppies.

I would love that I could be with you and *tell* these stories, but we can't always sit together around the fire in the deep dark nights. So, I also write books (and facilitate the occasional workshop, somewhere). Everything I write has a strong current of myth. Oh, and myth is never fallacy. Its etymology is a story, so deep within memory and culture, that the creator is unknown. And even the stories I write, set in the theoretical year 2156, or a winter 13,000 seasons around the sun from now, are not made up. That would be impossible.

You will find repetition in some of the CONTEMPLATIONS because they were written at different times. Most are about remembering who we are now; who we've been that make us who we are now. LORE are stories that go deeply to within many winters around the sun in widdershins right up to just last month. Some will be known, like Grandmother's shepherd's pie recipes and others I sneak onto the table, almost hesitantly. WITCH is not the last thing I write, because I have also begun Mercy Reilly's story, the third in the Traveler Series (The

Quickening and The Shining Isle), about the Tuatha Dé Dannan in and about New Rathmore. It's set in 2025, after the food riots, and Robin is lost. Been bashed so many times, by coppers and arseholes, he's in hospital with a few broken bits. He has forgotten he is the child of Hunter, a forest god and Puck, his mother, once-mortal. He calls himself Shadow. But between him and Mercy, one nasty, cruel Unseelie fáidh is about to have his motive uncovered.

That's the plan for the future. If I, and the me of me that is 90% bacteria, stay in this shape a while longer.

WITCH is a grimoire for opening at any page. Getting comfy on a lonesome night, and remembering, wildlings, that we're all about the spells and wonder. I'm simply old enough, to have dug deep enough, to offer you a picnic you might not have tasted before.

I'm glad you came. And I wish you good health and great excitation. And love. That's the biggie.

ABOUT

Indigenous Catuvellauni woman, strongest of many threads on the loom, unrealized and sold at birth. A right bastard. Now an elder. A time traveler. On another note, she has been in print since 1987 and is an award-winning author and filmmaker, director and producer of stage and screen, mother, grandmother, scholar, deep ecologist, mythographer, feminist, witch and psychic.

Ly is a proud storyteller. Using pen, film, her own skin, Ly seeks to unravel untrustworthy stereotypes and convoluted myths that have been condoned without thought for their meant purpose, to long-decimated tribal cultures that have refused to be annihilated or fully assimilated into the common dye. For many she is way too much like trouble.

Photography Serenity Rebel, daughter, Melbourne, 2018

www.ingramcontent.com/pod-product-compliance
Ingram Content Group UK Ltd.
Pitfield, Milton Keynes, MK11 3LW, UK
UKHW021314180426
11947UKWH00015B/1219